"This is the best bridge-building book written on the subject of Israel, the Jewish people and the Church! Go on a journey with my friend Don Finto and learn how you, too, can receive God's heart for His purposes among the Jewish people."

James W. Goll, founder, Encounters Network, Prayer Storm and GET eSchool; international bestselling author, *The Seer*, *The Lifestyle of a Prophet* and many more

"One cannot read this very timely, truly life-changing book without receiving God's heart for the Jewish people. Every believer needs to read *Your People Shall Be My People*."

Cindy Jacobs, co-founder, Generals International

"I am grateful to my friend Don Finto for paying the price to give us this highly significant, informative, prophetic book. This is a message from the mind and heart of God. When Jews and Gentiles alike embrace these powerful truths, a significant advancement of the Kingdom of God will become inevitable."

Mrs. Joy Dawson, international Bible teacher and bestselling author

"Controversy surrounds God's plan for Israel. Don Finto presents a biblical and exciting perspective of God's heart toward the Holy Land. In doing so, he gives us a valuable and inspiring resource for winning our Jewish friends to Christ."

Francis Frangipane, Advancing Church Ministries; founding pastor (retired), River of Life Ministries

"Here is a book of passion with good theology. Don Finto is passionate for the fulfillment of the destiny of the Church, which includes being a key instrument for the salvation of Israel. I look forward to seeing great Kingdom gain through the widespread distribution of this book."

Daniel Juster, director, Tikkun International

"In the spirit of Ruth, Don Finto has expressed the passion of God for Naomi—the Jewish people rejected yet destined for eternal purposes. In humility and loving identification, Finto has expressed the hearts of Messianic Jews to our beloved non-Jewish brothers around the table of our Lord. Dramatically, Israel has returned from exile. Prophetically, this signals a coming rediscovery of Yeshua (Jesus) as our Messiah. Now is the time for the Jewish-Gentile partnership prophesied in the book of Ruth to be fulfilled. *Your People Shall Be My People* could be your doorway to take part in Israel's final redemption."

Eitan Shishkoff, founding director, Tents of Mercy,
Kiryat Yam, Israel

"In this critical hour when the eyes of the world are turned toward Israel through the events unfolding in that nation, it is essential that God's people understand the key place the Jewish people hold, not only in current affairs, but in the ongoing plan of God down through the centuries. You cannot read Don Finto's book without having your eyes opened to God's purposes for His covenantal people. This highly informative book will deeply touch your heart as you glimpse the heart of the Father for His people."

Jane Hansen Hoyt, president/CEO, Aglow International

"In a world so confused by bad doctrine and teaching regarding Israel and the Church, Pastor Don Finto stands out as a beacon of truth and a breath of very fresh air! I encourage you to carefully and prayerfully read this important work. I am certain you will come to the same conclusion Don has: God loves Israel, and so should those who say they love the God of Israel!"

Paul Wilbur, recording artist

YOUR PEOPLE
SHALL BE
MY
PEOPLE

UPDATED AND EXPANDED EDITION

YOUR PEOPLE
SHALL BE
MY
PEOPLE

HOW ISRAEL, THE JEWS
AND THE CHRISTIAN CHURCH WILL COME
TOGETHER IN THE LAST DAYS

DON FINTO

Chosen

a division of Baker Publishing Group
Minneapolis, Minnesota

© 2001, 2016 by Don Finto

Published by Chosen Books
11400 Hampshire Avenue South
Bloomington, Minnesota 55438
www.chosenbooks.com

Chosen Books is a division of
Baker Publishing Group, Grand Rapids, Michigan

Printed in the United States of America

ISBN 978-0-8007-9789-8

Library of Congress Control Number: 2015957347

Cover design by Rob Williams, InsideOutCreativeArts

Contents

Contents

Foreword

God has sent a few people into our lives to encourage us, rebuke us, direct us, teach us and above all, to love us and love us well! Don Finto is at the top of our list. And from this man, who not only married us and prayed our children into existence but also guided us on two tours of Israel, comes a work that is a celebration of his passions. Don is passionate for the Word, and he is passionate for God's people, both Jew and Gentile.

In these years since this book was first published in 2001, we have followed Papa Don's example and learned to love God's Chosen People more intentionally. We have visited the Land, given more generously, prayed more fervently for the peace of Jerusalem and taught our five children (and now eleven grandchildren!) to honor their Jewish heritage.

One of the joys of being parents is seeing our children walk into their destiny with God's call burning in their hearts, using their gifts and talents to honor Him. (As a spiritual father to many, Don knows all about that!) A couple of years ago, our eldest son, Ryan, co-wrote the lyrics of a song, "The Promise," that has been and is being fulfilled in our day:

Fear not, O Israel, for there is peace still to come
A Word to break the silence, a promise yet to bloom.
The promise to redeem us, One to free us
Break the silence, end the violence in our hearts.

Emmanuel is sure to find us soon,
   the mighty Root of Jesse, Star of Truth,
And bring our sons to glory, tell His story,
Heal the broken and restore thee to His name.

The star will guide us to the humble place,
   where Christ the King reveals His earthly face
And we will see, Emmanuel,
God is with us, God is for us, God is in us!
We will sing, Alleluia!

We pray that the revised version of this book will be used by the Lord to bring Jewish "pre-believers" to Himself and remove the scales from believers' eyes concerning the ongoing role of Israel in God's affairs. He opened *our* eyes through Don's teaching, and now we—and our children and grandchildren—pray with new vision and clarity for God's purposes to be fulfilled for Israel and for the nations. Together—Messianic Jew and Gentile believer—we will sing, "Alleluia!"

Debbie and Michael W. Smith,
singer/songwriter, Franklin, Tennessee

Acknowledgments

I owe a great debt of gratitude to my Jesus-believing Jewish brothers and sisters who have challenged, encouraged and often led me. It all started during the Jesus Movement of the '70s. I was pastoring a church in Nashville, and some of these hippies-turned-"Jesus freaks" were Jewish and members of "my flock." As they opened up Scripture, they began to realize that they were a fulfillment of the Prophets, that they were actually returning to the roots of their faith, that this Jesus whom they had so recently come to know was Yeshua, their longed-for Messiah, and that even the "New Testament" is a Jewish handbook about the arrival of their Messiah, who is also the Redeemer of all the nations. I was compelled to reread the Prophets, and to get acquainted with other Jewish believing leaders involved in the restoration of "synagogues" of Jewish believers and their Gentile covenant partners.

That's when I met Eitan Shishkoff, Dan Juster and Asher Intrater. They became my early "mentors in the movement." If some Jewish ministry wanted to visit Belmont, I would call to be sure that this was a trustworthy ministry. A few years later, David Rudolph joined their leadership team and *Tikkun* (the Hebrew word for "restoration") Ministries was born. I was asked to serve on their governing council.

About the same time, I joined Dan, David, Marty Waldman, John Dawson, Peter Hocken and others on the steering committee of Toward Jerusalem Council II, calling the Church to repent for their centuries of anti-Semitism and to embrace and encourage the return of Jewish believers in Jesus. I started frequenting the annual meetings of the Messianic Jewish Alliance of America (MJAA) and the Union of Messianic Jewish Congregations (UMJC), and met many of these "born-again Jews" from around this nation and even the nations. Yohanna Chernoff's *Born a Jew, Die a Jew* helped me to understand the birth pains of the movement. To all of these I am forever grateful.

In late 1996, I started the Caleb Company, named after the biblical Caleb, who was still taking his mountains into old age, was raising up generations behind him and was wholeheartedly devoted to the Lord all of his life. To all those early board members and supporters, thank you.

By the year 2000, I carried a message that had to be written. I was a communicator, but not a writer, but I knew a writer/editor— Anne Severance. She helped me put my passion into words, and *Your People Shall Be My People* was born.

My initial encouragers from the publishing field were Bill Greig II and Kyle Duncan with Regal Books / Gospel Light. I am very grateful that they took a risk on an unknown author.

The *Your People* book struck a nerve and began to be read by Jewish believers and Gentiles who were coming alive with their love for the Jewish people as I was. Marty Waldman, who was serving on the Promise Keepers board, was asked how to help Gentile leaders understand the need to partner with Jewish believers. He recommended that *Your People* should be given to pastors and leaders of ministries. Regal allowed us to publish 55,500 giveaway copies. Promise Keepers founder, Coach Bill McCartney, wrote a foreword, and these books have moved around the world.

Chosen Books / Baker Publishing Group, seeing the value of the message of the book, has now asked for a revised and expanded edition. I could not be happier to work with this highly esteemed publishing company.

I met Chosen's acquisitions editor, Jane Campbell, years ago, and have never ceased to see the Spirit of God at work in her. She is a woman of prayer and integrity, and wants only God's heart to be communicated.

I've had some strong intercessors through the years, praying me into deeper revelation. Martha, my bride of now 64-plus years, is among them. She attends a weekly prayer meeting with a group of "good sisters" who have been meeting together for over 25 years! They know how to love, and they know how to pray. For them, I am perpetually grateful.

What more can I say? I am loved by the Eternal One. I am continually overwhelmed at His goodness, His forgiveness, His love, His Holy Spirit guidance. Jesus is my Forever Strength.

Introduction

The biblical story of Ruth is much more than the beautiful love story of King David's great-grandparents. Ruth is the symbol of every Gentile who has ever come to faith through Israel's God. The words of this Moabitess to her Jewish mother-in-law, Naomi— "Your people shall be my people and your God my God"—are a challenge to every non-Jew who believes in Boaz and Ruth's promised Son, Messiah, who would come down through their lineage. Every Gentile believer has come from the land of famine to the spiritual realm of abundance in that Name. Even Jesus' reference to Himself as the Bread of Life hearkens back to this ancient love story—to say nothing of the fact that He was born in the shadow of the very fields where Ruth was gleaning, just outside Beth-Lehem ("House of Bread").

But the Church through the centuries has not responded to her Boaz as Ruth responded to hers. The Church did not leave her Moabitish ways behind when she came into the house. Although she may have taken the "Bread" of Boaz, which represents Jesus to us, she turned her back on all His relatives, the Jewish people.

For eighteen centuries we rejected Boaz's (Jesus') near of kin. We forbade their godly heritage. They could no longer circumcise and Bar Mitzvah their sons, celebrate their God-ordained feasts or observe their Sabbaths. Those who insisted on remaining Jewish (sons and daughters of "Boaz") were ostracized, castigated, excommunicated or even killed.

Praise God, things are changing in our generation! Believers from the nations are reclaiming the biblical Jewish roots of their faith. Those from the nations are welcoming Jewish people back into the family of Jesus-followers. Ruth never claimed to be a Jew by ancestry, just as most of those from the nations are not trying to be Jewish, but they understand that the heritage of the Jewish people is the heritage of all believers. The feasts are not just Jewish feasts, they are "feasts of the Lord"—feasts that still have meaning for all of us who recognize the Jewish Messiah as our Redeemer.

Until I began to get this message, I had no desire to write a book. During the revival of the Jesus Movement when our congregation was flourishing, I was repeatedly asked to write, but I saw no reason to write. Better scribes were saying the same things I would say.

That changed in the late '90s when I "entered the world" of the Jewish believers in Jesus, reread the Prophets and the apostolic writings and began to see something that I did not find in print. Three core messages were pulsating within me and became the dominant message of the book: (1) According to the Prophets, our day is the day for Jewish eyes to open to their Messiah; (2) their return to the Land and to the Lord is triggering a world revival of mammoth proportions and (3) the Church is beginning to understand God's heart for His firstborn son, Israel, and is coming under the blessing of this united "one new man"—Jew and Gentile together.

During the writing, I was visiting with a pastor who, though passionately pursuing the Lord and desiring to know His Word, knew nothing of God's purposes for Israel. The Prophets had been like closed books for him, telling only the story of what had already been fulfilled. Until recently my friend had never considered reading the Prophets to find events now happening or yet to come.

He, as I did in earlier years, had taken clear words of Scripture about Israel's future and applied them to the Church, or had assigned these rich storehouses of prophetic treasure to the dusty bins of already fulfilled history. After our conversation, this young pastor began a fresh reading of biblical prophecy. He wants to know what he has missed! It is for such men and women that I have written.

About the same time, I received a letter from a pastor friend of mine who had no understanding of what I now believed to have discovered. We were reading the same Book, but had come up with completely different conclusions. "Jesus of Nazareth was the fulfillment of the Old Covenant and the end of God's preparatory people, the children of Israel," he wrote. "There is no such thing as a Messianic Jewish community. . . . The Kingdom of God is not fulfilled in an apostate people who are descendants by blood instead of by the seed which is only through faith. . . . The Christian church today is awash in this type of teaching, and you will rarely meet someone as old-fashioned as I who believes it to be false teaching and a corruption of Scripture."

I love this man even though I strongly disagree with him and even believe that people who hold such a view will be deceived as we move more and more into the final generation.

I am grateful to men and women of God through the centuries who have carved a path for people like me. As they read the Prophets, they began to believe that Israel would one day be a nation again, and that when they began coming to faith in Jesus, a great revival would be birthed throughout the world. As Peter so aptly put it in the first century, these men and women of God "searched intently and with the greatest care, trying to find out the time and circumstances to which the Spirit of Christ in them was pointing" (1 Peter 1:10–11), as they pondered the Prophets.

My experience in the Messianic movement has brought me to a clearer understanding of Jewish hearts, an awareness I do not find among many Christian pastors. I am passionate about seeing that my Jewish brothers and sisters are accepted as Jewish and encouraged to express their faith within a Jewish framework. I want to see the Gentile Church appreciating her own Jewish foundation stones. I want her to understand why Israel and the Jewish people are center stage in world history again, and I want her to be grateful for a returning Jewish leadership in the Body of Messiah.

As the Church understands the prophetic times in which we live, we will become better partners with God in hastening the fulfillment. We will confess personally and on behalf of the Church for the centuries of persecution of Jewish people and will become ardent intercessors on their behalf, looking for every opportunity to bless and not curse them.

In order to make this book more accurate in the context of our Jewish roots, I have chosen to use terms that are meaningful to both Jew and Gentile. For example, I will not use the word *church* in reference to congregations of Jewish believers: first of all, because the word *church* is not the best translation of the Greek word *ekklesia*, often carrying with it the idea of a building rather than a group of people, and second of all, because Jewish assemblies will more often use the word *congregation* (an equally good translation of the Greek *ekklesia*, literally "the called-out ones"). In this book you will find "Church" capitalized when the meaning is the Gentile Church at large.

Most of the time I will refer to *the Messiah* rather than to the Christ. That is because I have chosen to use the translation from the Hebrew rather than the Greek. *Christ,* for many Jewish people, has become a hated word, since many of the atrocities leveled against them have been perpetrated in that name. And even for those in the Church, the word *Christ* has become almost like Jesus' last name, with no particular meaning.

Conversion is not a word you will find me using as it relates to Jewish people. We from the nations are the ones who converted to Israel's God, the God of creation, the God of Abraham, Isaac and Jacob. I want my Jewish brothers and sisters to be restored to their own God and their Promised Messiah. Yes, in the sense of turning, they "convert," but that word carries such a weight of persecution because of the forced "conversions" of the past.

Nor will you often see me referring to Jesus-followers as "Christians," since that word no longer carries the original idea of Christ-followers. There are "Christians" who do not believe Jesus rose from the dead. There are "Christians" who do not accept the Prophets and apostolic writings as the Word of God. "Christians" have been the greatest persecutors of the Jewish people, and the early believers did not use that word to describe themselves.[1] They referred to themselves as followers of "the Way" (Acts 24:14).

I personally enjoy using Jesus' Hebrew name, Yeshua, because that would be the name by which Miriam (Mary), His Jewish mother, referred to Him. Realizing that this term may seem strange to many readers, I have used these two names almost interchangeably.

Sometimes I refer to the Jews, but even this name—a derivative of Judah, Israel's dominant tribe in the southern Kingdom and Jesus' own tribe—has taken on negative connotations for the Jewish people. I have rarely heard a Jewish person introduce himself or herself with the words "I am a Jew." Rather, they say, "I am Jewish." Therefore, in this book, I speak often of the Jewish people rather than the Jews. I love the Jewish people and will do whatever is necessary to make my speech more acceptable to this persecuted, closest blood family of our Lord.

These are some of the thoughts that have motivated me to share my heart. I have never considered myself a writer, and yet I believe I am seeing things that have not been written or widely circulated. I invite you to hear me out prayerfully and, like the Bereans mentioned by Luke in Acts 17:11, search the Scriptures to see if I am correct.

Listen to Ruth, our non-Jewish covenant partner, as she speaks to her Jewish mother-in-law: "Wherever you go, I will go; and wherever you lodge, I will lodge; your people shall be my people, and your God, my God" (1:16 NKJV).

Could this be the covenant pledge we must make with the Jewish people? If you agree, may your life never be the same! May you become a zealous advocate of Israel and Israel's children, fervently pleading their case before the Father's throne . . . just as my colleague, Tod McDowell, now pleads in their behalf. . . .

Remarks from Tod McDowell, director, Caleb Company

I met Don Finto on February 4, 2005. He was sitting in the courtyard of the Visitors' Center of Youth With A Mission's (YWAM) largest training campus in Kona, Hawaii. He wasn't what I expected. He had a smile that made me feel accepted and comfortable immediately. His youthful exuberance and childlike humility drew me in. What made this man tick? What was it that caused such life and love to emanate from him?

As I sat down on the plastic chair, my mind flashed back to three days earlier. My phone had rung with a call from Australia, a number I didn't recognize. I was on the 33rd day of a 40-day fast, seeking keys to global revival. I had been in YWAM, the world's largest mission organization, for thirteen years, serving on the president's council, teaching in their School of Biblical Studies, leading outreach teams all over the world, and had recently begun a worship and intercession team called IGNITE.

But I was yearning for more of God's heart. I had withdrawn from ministry for a season so that I could spend my days in fasting and prayer. I met with my IGNITE team once a week, but had asked not to be called unless there was some unusual need. The phone call was, therefore, unexpected.

"Hello, Tod!" came the voice on the other end of the line as I reluctantly took the call. "Tod, I love what you are doing, and totally agree with the revelation the Lord is giving you. Worship and intercession are indeed core essentials for world revival, but I believe you are missing a piece. You need to get the 'Israel piece.'"

Stunned, I pressed my caller for more.

"You need to read this book by Don Finto, *Your People Shall Be My People*," she said.

"Interesting," I responded. "I actually have that book. It was given to me, but I have yet to read it." I thanked my friend for the call and hung up the phone, pondering, praying.

What is this all about, Lord? Why would she feel the necessity to call? Don't I know more about world revival than she? Yet I trust her as an intercessor. (Her two children were a part of our IGNITE team.) *Lord, what's going on?*

Still a bit shaken by the whole encounter, I received another phone call about an hour later, this time from one of the school leaders over which I had oversight. "Tod, please excuse me for calling," she said, "but I really believe the Lord wanted me to call. We have a guest speaker on campus this week, and I felt that you may want to get with him. He has a free day on Friday. His name is Don Finto."

Now I am doubly stunned.

And so, on this Friday morning at eleven o'clock, I am sitting with Don as he is giving me his best PowerPoint for believing that our relationship with Israel and the Jewish people is a key for world revival. What he was saying was interesting, but not necessarily life-changing until he hit Romans 11:12.

"If their [Jewish] transgression means riches for the world, and their [Jewish] loss means riches for the Gentiles [the nations], how much greater riches will their fullness bring?"

"Wait a minute!" I said, as that verse sprang alive within me. "I believe there is something here that I need. Would you pray for me?"

Tears welled up in my eyes as I knelt, Don kneeling beside me. Soon I was facedown, weeping, asking God to speak to me and tell me what was happening. All I heard in my spirit was, "You are married to the Jewish people."

Married to the Jewish people? Is Rachel Jewish? Lord, what are You trying to tell me?

Then I realized that if God is in covenant with the Jewish people, then I also am in covenant with the Jewish people.

Later on that Friday evening, we were in a campus dinner where Don was present before returning to Nashville the next day. I introduced him to Rachel and the children, and we spent perhaps fifteen minutes together. We were both impacted by the time together, but neither of us had any expectancy of ever being together again. . . .

And so it was that over ten years ago, we began a spiritual father/son relationship. The reading of this book helped my mind catch up with the revelation the Spirit had given regarding our covenant relationship with Israel and the Jewish people. Over eight years ago, my family and I moved to Nashville. I am now the director of the Caleb Company, which Don started in 1996. Don and I talk or see each other almost daily: praying, ministering, traveling and strategizing together. It is a great privilege to partner with him in building the kingdom through "equipping God's people with His heart and purpose for Israel and the nations."

The Beginning of the End

> When these things begin to take place, stand up and lift up
> your heads, because your redemption is drawing near.
>
> Luke 21:28

God promised Abraham, "I will make you into a great nation and I will bless you; I will make your name great, and you will be a blessing. I will bless those who bless you, and whoever curses you I will curse; and all peoples on earth will be blessed through you" (Genesis 12:2–3). If this ancient promise is still true, and it is, then no person, no congregation, no nation or people group will ever receive their fullest blessing until they learn to love the Jewish people.

I have not always been so passionate about this truth. Let me tell you why I believe these are prophecy-fulfilling times in which we live and how I, a West Texas farm boy, became involved in the Messianic Jewish community and came to love this covenant people.

In the early '50s, my wife, Martha, and I were fresh out of college, newlyweds and ministering in postwar Germany. The nation was disgraced and divided; homes and neighborhoods were emotionally and physically destroyed. We were young and idealistic and wanted to be a part of directing this humbled people back to God.

As a Bible major in a Christian college, I graduated confident of what I believed. I knew how to read the Bible to overlook certain passages and to interpret others so that they always said what I had been taught. We knew that any other understanding of Scripture would separate us from close friends and family. Occasionally this would make me uncomfortable. I would read Scripture that did not quite fit what I had been taught. But after all, my professors, who were godly men, knew better than I. They read Hebrew and Greek, and they could not be wrong.

Then the postcard arrived. I remember it as if it were yesterday.

I hated that card! It embarrassed me. It challenged me. It rattled me. I thought the young man who had sent it, a freshman student at the University of Hamburg, to be extremely arrogant. I showed the card to no one, not even to Martha. I tore it up and discarded the pieces almost immediately.

And yet I could not forget it. I can still quote it almost verbatim: *"Lieber Don Finto, liest Du die Bibel, um zu sehen, was die Bibel sagt, oder liest Du sie nur, um eine Predigt vorzubereiten?"* "Dear Don Finto, do you ever read the Bible to find out what it says, or do you just read it to prepare a sermon?" The card was signed "Helmut."

I read the Bible regularly, but I knew at the core of my being that I often studied the Bible to defend positions already held rather than studying to see if these positions were biblically accurate. Did I really want to know God's heart on every issue? Would I be willing to change my belief even if it meant estrangement from those who were closest to me? I desired that of others. What about myself? For the next several years, Helmut's card held me accountable and was a constant reminder to ask the Lord for understanding.

Meeting the Author

After eight years in Germany, Martha and I returned to the United States, where I continued with educational pursuits that enabled me to begin teaching German and some Bible courses in a Christian college. The charismatic movement was sweeping the nation, and many people were rethinking long-held beliefs. This was also the beginning of the hippie years that resulted in the Jesus Movement of the late '60s and early '70s. I was not interested in becoming a part of a new movement, but I did have a growing hunger to know God, to know Jesus, to know the Holy Spirit. I knew the Book rather well, but I did not know the Author intimately.

Almost two decades after receiving Helmut's card, while teaching in that college in Nashville, Tennessee, I was also preaching for one of the local congregations where a retired dentist often attended. Dr. Hall was a student of prophecy. He delved into the biblical prophets, Isaiah to Malachi, as well as the prophecy of the New Covenant Scriptures. Dr. Hall began inviting me to lunch so that we could discuss Scripture. After a few lunches together, he began probing me about my understanding of biblical prophecy: How much did I read the Prophets? Did I ever let the Old Testament prophets speak for themselves, or had I just presumed that everything they had written had already been fulfilled at the first coming of Jesus?

Flashes of Helmut's card!

I felt temporarily trapped by Dr. Hall's probing questions.

I had read the Bible for years, but I had read the Hebrew Scriptures primarily as history. In my annual reading through the Bible, I was always relieved to get to the New Testament. The ancient prophets spoke so often of Moab and Babylon, of Ephraim and Edom, and I, not being an astute student of history, understood very little of it. Except for those occasional clear words that foretold Jesus' coming, I would almost speed-read the Prophets in order to get through them.

25

If I did run across something about Israel's return to the Land, I assumed that this was speaking of her return from Babylon. (Somehow I overlooked the fact that these passages mentioned returning not only from the East [Babylon] but also from the West [the Americas] and from the North [Turkey, Ukraine, Russia] and South [Ethiopia and all of Africa]—from the nations.) In those verses that told of the Messiah reigning over all the earth, I assumed the Prophets were speaking symbolically and meant the advance of the Gospel. If I did not understand a passage, I either ignored it or spiritualized it. "Israel" was the Church. "Israel's sins" were the sins of the Church. "Jerusalem" was a figure of heaven. "Zion" was another name for the people of God.

Stirred by Dr. Hall's challenge, I began to reread the Prophets. This resulted in more questions than answers. There was no place in my theology for a regathering of Israel. I had never even considered that there might be a time when most or all of the Jewish people would recognize their Messiah. I had been taught that Jesus would never again return to the earth. It never occurred to me that some of the prophecies might literally be fulfilled—that the Lord would again stand on the Mount of Olives and that the mountain would split in two, exactly as Zechariah saw it (see Zechariah 14:4).

The Great Debate

I was faced with a dilemma. What is to be taken literally in the Scriptures and what is mere symbolism?

I decided that I would rather assume that the Bible is literally true and then be proven wrong in that assumption than to assume it is symbolism and be wrong. I prefer to meet the Lord one day and say, "I took You at Your Word" than to meet Him and have to admit that I didn't think He meant what He said.

It seemed best to take the Scriptures literally unless the Scriptures themselves suggested otherwise. There were times when Jesus would expressly say, "The kingdom of heaven is *like* . . ." That's figurative language. Even in the book of Revelation, John often speaks of a "sign" appearing in the heavens (12:1), while at other times he speaks of seeing an actual new heaven and a new earth or a Holy City coming down from God out of heaven (see 21:1–2).

This literal approach to the reading of prophecy began to change my understanding of the Jewish situation. Passages that I had long allegorized now had to be more carefully discerned. For example, Ezekiel's "valley of dry bones" (Ezekiel 37) is not just a good sermon to preach to a dead church, but it is exactly what the prophet said it was—a picture of Israel coming back to life (verses 12–13). To accept the Scripture allegorically without accepting the actual prophecy is to thwart the full purpose of God's Word, to twist it to suit one's own agenda.

Once we have accepted the prophet Ezekiel's literal meaning— that Israel will live again—then we can apply that passage to other situations. This kind of openness to the Word of God keeps the Scriptures alive. The Lord, through His Spirit, continually brings fresh revelation, both the literal meaning and the spiritual applications.

We do not have the right to take words spoken to Israel and appropriate them to the Church until we have recognized their intended meaning to the people originally addressed. Even then, these promises belong to us, the Gentile Church, only because we are grafted in to Israel's roots and, along with her, inherit the promises made to her. Paul says that we have become a part of Israel's olive tree "among the others" and "share in the nourishing sap from the olive root" (Romans 11:17). We do not replace the originally intended recipients. The promise of salvation is extended "to all Abraham's offspring—not only to those who are of the law but also to those who are of the faith of Abraham" (Romans 4:16). Not only, but also! We join the family of Abraham and are "fellow citizens with God's people" (Ephesians 2:19). The Jewish Messiah has become our Messiah. His blood has also redeemed us. We come alongside Israel in receiving the promises, but we do not *replace* her!

27

I was having difficulty in discerning the meaning of prophecy, not unlike most of the people in Jesus' day. The keepers of the scrolls did not understand their meaning. Those who were looking for the Messiah did not recognize Him. They were too preoccupied with preconceived perceptions of what the Messiah would do, of what He would be like. He stood before them in the flesh, but their eyes were closed. I was, in truth, no different.

The Scriptures were clear enough. Micah called Bethlehem the place of His origin (see Micah 5:2). Zebulun and Naphtali in Galilee were singled out by Isaiah as a place that would see "a great light" (Isaiah 9:1–2). Zechariah knew the price for which Jesus would be betrayed (see Zechariah 11:12–13). Isaiah foretold that Jesus would be a suffering servant (see Isaiah 53). Zechariah wrote of a donkey that would be involved in His arrival (see Zechariah 9:9). Daniel even predicted the exact season when the "Anointed One, the ruler" would come (9:25). These predictions may be clear to us today, but the religious leaders of Jesus' day missed them, because He did not live up to their preconceived expectations.

"You diligently study the Scriptures because you think that by them you possess eternal life. These are the Scriptures that testify about me," Jesus told His hearers (John 5:39). His implication is that they would have recognized Him if they had believed their own Scriptures. These were Bible teachers who were obviously reading not to learn what Scripture taught, but to prove what they believed to be true!

The Revelation That Comes from the Spirit

Intellectual honesty alone is not sufficient when we are seeking to know God. We must pray that our eyes will be open, that our hearts will be perceptive. We must yearn for insight and revelation. He not only speaks to the mind, but He also reveals Himself to the spirit. That revelation comes in His timing. We must be willing, but He is the One who reveals. We may read through Scripture again and again and miss the truth if our hearts and our spiritual eyes have not been opened.

Cleopas and his friend had a problem on the Emmaus Road on resurrection morning. They were looking into the face of Jesus, but they did not recognize Him (see Luke 24:16). Not until the veil was removed from their eyes did they know with whom they were speaking. We need our veils removed!

Lydia had a similar experience at the riverbank prayer meeting just outside Philippi. As Paul began to speak, "the Lord opened her heart to respond to Paul's message" (Acts 16:14). Lydia had to be willing, but without that opening of her heart, she would not have been able to receive.

Do you see why Paul cried out to the Ephesians that "the eyes of your heart may be enlightened" (1:18) and that God "may give you the Spirit of wisdom and revelation, so that you may know him better" (verse 17)? "The mind controlled by the Spirit" is that which brings "life and peace," Paul told the Romans (8:6).

God does not speak English or German or Japanese, not even Hebrew. He speaks "spirit." Rarely does He speak audibly through our outside ears, but inwardly where He dwells. He speaks to us in our spirits through His Spirit. We do not translate His messages; rather we interpret them (see 1 Corinthians 14:13). Revelation goes deeper than the mind. It impacts the entire being—mind, heart, intention, passions. This is why Paul told the Romans that their salvation had come by believing "in your heart" that God had raised Jesus from the dead (Romans 10:9), that "it is with your heart that you believe and are justified" (verse 10).

Luke 21 and the Present-Day Move of God

It was this kind of searching that caused me to hear God's heart for Israel. The beginning of the revelation happened in the early

'70s, when I was studying the gospel of Luke with a group of young people. Students were packed into a storefront classroom. They were sitting on the floor, Bibles open on their laps, hungry to know more of this Jesus whom they had so recently met. They had few preconceived ideas. They were reading the Bible afresh and asking the Lord for revelation.

For weeks we had been reading together through Luke's account of the life of Jesus, wanting to know more of Him so that we could become more like Him. The Lord was revealing Himself to us—both to me, the teacher, and to these radical young believers.

Everything was going along well until the week we came to Luke 21. I began to dread this particular class session because I did not know how to understand this chapter, much less interpret it for others. In this passage, and the corresponding chapters in Matthew 24 and Mark 13, the Lord had been talking to the disciples about the future—His future and the future of Israel. According to Matthew's account of the same conversation, Jesus was answering three questions from the disciples: (1) When will the destruction of Jerusalem come? (2) What will be the sign of Your coming? and (3) What will be the sign of the end of the age? (see Matthew 24:3). Jesus seems to be answering all three questions, but I could not comprehend which answer belonged to which question.

I was rereading the chapter one last time in front of my eager students when I began to see—on the spot—something pertinent to our day. The Lord was giving me a revelation that has been foundational to my understanding of the times ever since.

Suddenly four verses seemed strikingly clear. Luke 21:20 surely speaks of the armies of Titus: "When you see Jerusalem being surrounded by armies, you will know that its desolation is near." The Roman armies began their assault of Jerusalem in AD 68 and continued until its fall and the destruction of the Temple in AD 70. Jesus had wept over the city and the leaders' lack of receptivity.

Verse 24 speaks of the dispersion of the Jews: "They [the Jewish people] will fall by the sword and will be taken as prisoners *to all the nations*" (italics added). This happened just as Jesus said it would. Many thousands died in the siege. Others fled the city, never to return. They would soon be found in every nation of the world. Some returned to Jerusalem a few years later but were driven out again during the Bar Kokhba revolt of the 130s.[1]

After the Romans successfully crushed the Bar Kokhba campaign, Jewish people were banned from Jerusalem and from Judea. Although there were times in the ensuing years when Jews were allowed to live in the city and in the Land, there was no further serious Jewish occupation until the beginning of immigration in the nineteenth century. There was no Jewish State until the United Nations' vote of November 1947 led to the establishment of the modern State of Israel in May 1948![2]

"Jerusalem will be trampled on by the Gentiles," Jesus went on to say in verse 24. And what trampling! Romans, Byzantines, Muslims, Crusaders, Turks, the British—all have claimed time and territory in the City of David, in this Land promised to Abraham and his descendants.

"Until the times of the Gentiles are fulfilled!" I paused in the reading, deep in thought. What a strange thing for the Jewish Messiah to say. What could this possibly have meant to Jesus' hearers that day? The Land had been in Israel's possession, more or less, since the days of Joshua. Yes, some had been taken to Assyria in 721 BC and had never returned. Others were held captive in Babylon for seventy years in the sixth century BC. But even in those times, Jews still lived in the Land.

Whatever Jesus meant by "times of the Gentiles," one thing was clear: Israel's reentry into Jerusalem was strangely connected to these words in Luke 21. As I read, the modern history of Israel was merging with Scripture. The people now returning to the Land were descendants of those who had heard the words I was now reading!

Jesus had said "until." I was suddenly confident that the "until" referred to the recent past when, in the Six-Day War of June 1967, the State of Israel held off six invading Arab nations and recaptured the city of Jerusalem. This was the first sovereign possession of the city of Jerusalem since 586 BC, when the last Jewish king in David's lineage was driven from the city.[3]

In the margin of my Bible, I wrote "1967." If this Scripture had found its fulfillment in Israel's retaking of Jerusalem, then "the times of the Gentiles" also had meaning for our generation.

Sitting on the floor in front of me that day were not only Gentile believers in Jesus but also young Jewish believers who had accepted Yeshua (Jesus), the One whom Moses, Isaiah, Jeremiah, Micah and the other prophets had promised. I had been hearing of an influx of Jewish believers like no other since the first century. Somehow I knew this was significant for our day.

I read on.

In verse 28, Jesus said to His listeners, "When these things begin to take place, stand up and lift up your heads, because your redemption is drawing near."

I was having a "this is that!" experience—the kind of surreal moment that occurred when Jesus read from the Isaiah text in the synagogue at Nazareth. "Today this scripture is fulfilled in your hearing," He had said (Luke 4:21). I wanted to tell my young floor-sitting friends and all others who would listen to me since that time, "This Scripture is being fulfilled in our day!" I wanted to shout like Peter did on Pentecost morning, "This is that which was spoken by the prophet Joel"! (Acts 2:16 KJV). I was experiencing what Jesus had declared!

The fulfillment of Luke 21 had begun. I was seeing the beginning of the end. I was to stand up and lift up my head; our redemption was near.

But what is "near"? I don't know. The Lord does not reckon time as we do. "Near" may be many years, or it may be tomorrow.

The last verse to catch my attention was verse 32: "This generation will certainly not pass away until all these things have happened." What generation? The generation at the time of Jesus?

No, that cannot be, since that generation is long since gone. The generation that begins to see these things being fulfilled? I think so.

But how long is a generation? I don't have a definitive answer to that question, either. The Lord led Israel through the wilderness for forty years and called it a generation. Yet He told Moses that the Israelites would come back to the Promised Land "in the fourth generation" (Genesis 15:16). That return took 400 years. So a generation could be 100 years. If my understanding of "this generation" is correct, then some of us who were alive when Israel took control of Jerusalem will still be alive when Jesus returns.

One thing is certain: He promised that all these things will occur, and I believe Him.

Signs of His Coming

But wait, you may be saying, we are not supposed to be involved in date-setting for the Second Coming, are we? Didn't Jesus Himself say, "No one knows about that day or hour, not even the angels in heaven, nor the Son, but only the Father" (Matthew 24:36)? Have there not been hundreds of prognosticators, all of whom have been proven wrong? Didn't Jesus say that His coming would be like a thief in the night? Does He really want us to know the season of His return?

Yes and no.

No, we are not to know the day or the hour.

Yes, hundreds of prognosticators have been proven wrong.

But yes, we are to know the season of His return. Jesus chided the leaders of His day for being able to discern weather signs, but not "the signs of the times" (Matthew 16:3).

Yes, Jesus is coming like a thief in the night for those who are not expecting His return. "You know very well that the day of the Lord will come like a thief in the night," Paul told the

33

Thessalonians (1 Thessalonians 5:2). "While people are saying, 'Peace and safety,' destruction will come on them suddenly, as labor pains on a pregnant woman" (verse 3). While people are saying, "Peace and safety!" destruction will come on them!

No, Jesus will not come like a thief in the night for believers. "You . . . are not in darkness so that this day should surprise you like a thief," Paul continued (verse 4). "If you do not wake up, I will come like a thief, and you will not know at what time I will come to you," Jesus told the community in Sardis (Revelation 3:3).

"As it was in the days of Noah, so it will be at the coming of the Son of Man" (Matthew 24:37), were Jesus' words. How was it in the days of Noah?

Noah, warned of God, was not surprised when the rains came. He and his family knew that they were living in the season of the coming judgment. Though they had never experienced a flood, the ark was built and ready. The animals "came to Noah and entered the ark" (Genesis 7:9). Noah might not have known exactly when the floodwaters would come, but he knew the season.

And what was that about the coming of Jesus compared to the labor pains of a pregnant woman?

Labor pains come as no surprise to a pregnant woman. She has been expecting them for nine months. She still does not know the hour or the day of her child's arrival, not even when the pains begin. But she knows that her time is near. This, according to Paul, is how it will be at the coming of the Son of Man. We will know the season, though not the day nor the hour.

Jesus spoke of many signs that would occur through the centuries before the time of the end. Most of these have happened in every generation—floods, famines, plagues. They may be coming with greater frequency, but they are not new. They alone are insufficient clues regarding the season in which we are living.

Paul told Timothy that the end times would usher in a period of intense brutality, of civil and family unrest, of increased addictions (lack of self-control), a time when the whole world would be seeking after pleasure. Even the Body of Christ would have "a form of godliness but denying its power" (see 2 Timothy 3:1–5). These signs, too, have been present in former generations.

But since my encounter with Luke 21 that day in front of my floor-sitting, "Jesus freak" friends, I am convinced that one sign is unique to our day: Israel is back in the Land of her inheritance, and Jerusalem is once again under the rule of the nation of Israel, just as the prophets and Jesus foretold.

Jesus spoke of many signs that would occur before the end times. One sign is unique to our day—Israel is back in the Land and Jerusalem is once again under the rule of the nation of Israel.

When Jesus was predicting the fall of Jerusalem, He wept over the city:

O Jerusalem, Jerusalem, you who kill the prophets and stone those sent to you, how often I have longed to gather your children together, as a hen gathers her chicks under her wings, but you were not willing. . . . I tell you, you will not see me again until you say, "Blessed is he who comes in the name of the Lord."

Matthew 23:37, 39

This word was not spoken to the Gentiles. It was spoken to Jesus' blood family, Israel. He would not return until the Jewish people, perhaps Jewish leaders in Jerusalem, were ready to receive Him. With the eyes of faith, we can see that time approaching.

I have been to Israel many times in the past twenty years. I have stood on the Mount of Olives with Jewish believers, gazing into the sky and praying, anticipating the Lord's return, crying out to the heavens, "Blessed is He who comes in the name of the Lord!"

No generation since the first century has seen such a rapidly increasing body of Jewish believers, both in the Land and in the nations. The "until" Jesus spoke when overlooking Jerusalem that day shortly before His death is drawing nearer. We are seeing Jewish people who are ready to embrace their Messiah—Jewish people who are ready to say, "Blessed is He who comes in the name of the Lord."

Walk with me through some of the truths I have learned since that day with my hippie/Jesus Movement class of young Jewish and Gentile believers. Let me tell you about other prophecies that are unfolding before us—recorded words of the Prophets that looked forward to our day.

If you question what I am saying, take "my" Scriptures and test them for yourself. Open your Bible and read. Ask the Lord to open your heart and mind and spirit. Leave behind preconceptions of the biblical record. Let the Lord speak to you. Ask for revelation. Seek wisdom. Be willing to be changed!

My own focus is sharpening. God's heart for the Jewish people must be my heart for them. As our hearts turn with the longing He has for this specially called family, you and I will find ourselves under that age-old blessing spoken to Abraham, and our spirits will be quickened to read the global signs of the Messiah's imminent return to claim all of His children—Jew and Gentile alike.

Remarks from Skyler Fox,
former student, Caleb Training School

I grew up in a family that believed we are living in the last days before the Lord's return. This was always something that resonated in my heart, even though I had no absolute confirmation that this was true—not until my time in the Caleb Company Training School.

As "Papa Don" began to refer to Jesus' prophecy about the destruction of Jerusalem—that the Jewish people would be "taken as prisoners to all the nations" and that Jerusalem would be "trampled on by the Gentiles until the times of the Gentiles are fulfilled" (Luke 21:24), I began to pay attention. All my life I had heard of the Jewish return to Israel, and Israel's retaking of their capital city in 1967. Suddenly I realized that Jesus' prediction had been fulfilled in our day.

Then Papa Don moved to verse 28 of Jesus' discourse: "When these things begin to take place, stand up and lift up your heads, because your redemption is drawing near."

Now my attention was riveted on what I was hearing. Yes, these things have begun to take place. Yes, this means that our redemption is near. Yes, we are living in the season of Jesus' return.

But what exactly does that mean? How long is the season? What is near? That's when I saw Jesus' further explanation: "When you see these things happening, you know that the kingdom of God is near. . . . This generation will certainly not pass away until all these things have happened" (verses 31–32).

I now walk confidently in the truth of the hour I live in. May His kingdom come on earth as it is in heaven!

The "Greater Riches"
World Revival

> If their transgression means riches for the world, and their
> loss means riches for the Gentiles, how much greater riches
> will their fullness bring!
>
> Romans 11:12

I was never the same after my revelation from Luke 21. Although
I continued to pastor a church, I remained alert to Jewish issues. I
read every book, newspaper and magazine I could find pertaining
to this subject. Israel was then, as it is now, almost daily on the
evening news. My heart was irresistibly drawn to Jewish people. At
times I was overcome with grief for this people who had endured
the wrath of the nations for so many centuries. All my studies in
many passages in the Scriptures, both Old Covenant and New,
drove me to examine all data from this perspective.

We are told that over half of the people who have ever lived
on the earth since the days of Adam and Eve are alive today. The

latest figures indicate that one out of every five of these is a believer—more believers today than in all the years preceding us.[1]
Millions of people on every continent are coming to faith—the
greatest revival in the history of the world!

The revival that is sweeping the world is not often seen in the
West, for centuries the bastion of the faith, but in nations long
closed to the Gospel of Jesus. China is an excellent example. We
have met some of the leaders of the Chinese movement in recent
months, rejoicing over the 80 to 100 million Chinese who have
come to faith in Jesus in spite of the sometimes intense persecution, imprisonment and even death. One of the Chinese leaders
spoke up and corrected us: "One hundred *forty* million!" he said.
Since then we have heard reports as high as 175 million. According to YWAM's (Youth With A Mission's) figures, 1,200 Chinese
per hour are coming to faith.[2] That's over 10 million a year. Fifty
years ago there were no more than 1 million believers in that vast
country. Why? How can we explain such a dramatic increase in
the harvest of souls?

In 1948, when the State of Israel was born, China, with its 1 million believers, was about to come under Communist rule. Pastors
and leaders were imprisoned or killed, and church buildings were
destroyed. The Church was forced to go underground. But the
Church did not die. By the time of Israel's Jubilee fifty years later,
when Westerners were able to contact the underground Church,
they found a thriving community of faith—80 million strong. That
alone is an increase of 8,000 percent!

Often these awakenings come in the most unlikely places. From
the September/October 2008 issue of *Mission Frontiers,* a magazine
that serves the Center for World Missions, I learned of the revival
in Iran in spite of the fact that modern-day "Hitlers" have ruled
that nation with the express purpose of eradicating the world's
Jewish population. I learned that the awakening began in the 1960s
when a team of American missionaries had a passion to see the
contemporary population of Persia (Iran was formerly Persia) come

to know their Savior. One of their first disciples was assassinated for his faith, but not before the God-movement was out of control.

The young people of Iran wanted to read this forbidden Bible and learn about this forbidden Teacher named Jesus. The government forbade satellite dishes, but they were often smuggled into the country by the very officials who had forbidden them, and now Christian TV ranks among the top ten programs in Iran. Everyone seems to want a Bible. One woman has single-handedly given away 20,000 with no one ever refusing the gift.

One young man from Iran, with whom I have visited on Skype, is now living in Ukraine. Though raised in a devout Muslim family as a hater of Christians and the Jewish people, he was irresistibly drawn to faith and is now an ardent disciple of the Man from Nazareth. Today he owns a publishing company in Ukraine, and has been used of God to publish the *Your People* book in both Farsi and Arabic, offered without cost on the Internet.

Another unlikely place for the Gospel to penetrate is the Palestine territories, especially the refugee camps. Tass Saada tells his own story in the book *Once an Arafat Man*. Tass was born in Gaza and raised in Saudi Arabia in the world of radical Islam and violent Palestinian nationalism. By his own admission, he became a personal friend of Yasser Arafat and a persecutor of Christians and murderer of Jews, both civilians and soldiers. Tass's radicalism took an about-face when he became a follower of Jesus and began to get acquainted with Jewish people.

Joel Rosenberg, a former aide to Prime Minister Benjamin Netanyahu, wrote the foreword to Tass's book. Rosenberg calls Tass "a jihadist who found Jesus, a violent revolutionary who was radically transformed one day by the power of the Holy Spirit and became a man of peace and compassion . . . a man who fell in love with a Savior who loves Arabs as well as Jews. . . . Here we were, a former aide to top PLO Chairman Yasser Arafat and a former aide to Prime Minister Benjamin Netanyahu, hugging each other—not trying to kill each other—in the heart of Jerusalem.

41

All because of the work Jesus had done to give us hearts of love rather than hatred."[3]

What connection is there between these astonishing statistics and the Jewish people?

Robert Leighton, a Puritan of the seventeenth century, came to understand that connection. He wrote,

> They forget a main point for the Church's glory who pray not daily for the conversion of the Jews. Undoubtedly, that people of the Jews shall once more be commanded to arise and shine, and their return shall be the "riches of the Gentiles," and that shall be a more glorious time than ever the Church of God did yet behold![4]

These words, written over 350 years ago, posed a revolutionary concept in his day. For seventeen centuries the Church had assumed that God was finished with Israel, that the Church had replaced her. The Christian Church was now to be the recipient of all the promises formerly made to Israel.

Leighton must have been reading the "Jewish section" of the book of Romans (chapters 9–11) when he came upon a series of searing questions written by Paul: "Did God reject his people?" (11:1). "Did they stumble so as to fall beyond recovery?" (verse 11). "If their transgression means riches for the world, and their loss means riches for the Gentiles, how much greater riches will their fullness bring!" (verse 12). "If their rejection is the reconciliation of the world, what will their acceptance be but life from the dead?" (verse 15).

Wait a minute! Robert Leighton must have thought. *God is not through with the Jews! They are coming back. And according to Paul, when they do, it will mean the greatest harvest of souls the world has yet known! Greater riches! Life from the dead!*

Leighton understood Paul to be saying that world revival among the nations would parallel Israel's return to the Land and to the Lord. Robert Leighton was seeing prophetically what our generation is now experiencing.

Seeing in Advance

Robert Leighton's voice was not the only prophetic voice of earlier centuries that foretold the physical and spiritual restoration of Israel. As early as 1560, among the great English and Scottish Protestant leaders who produced the Geneva Bible, there was recognition of God's yet-to-be-fulfilled call on Israel. These men wrote in the marginal notes of Romans 11:15, 25: "He sheweth that the time shall come that the whole nation of the Jews, though not every one particularly, shall be joined to the church of Christ."[5]

In 1649, John Owen preached before the House of Commons, foretelling a time when "this ancient people" will come to be "one fold with the fullness of the Gentiles . . . in answer to millions of prayers. . . . There is not any promise anywhere of raising up a kingdom unto the Lord Jesus Christ in this world but it is either expressed, or clearly intimated, that the beginning of it must be with the Jews."[6]

In 1839, Robert Murray M'Cheyne, a Scottish Presbyterian, traveled to "Palestine" and returned home to preach a sermon based on Romans 1:16: "I am not ashamed of the gospel, because it is the power of God for the salvation of everyone who believes: first for the Jew, then for the Gentile."

Charles Simeon, Cambridge preacher from 1782 to 1836, once became so carried away with the future of the Jews that when a friend wrote him the question, "Six millions of Jews and six hundred millions of Gentiles—which is the most important?" Simeon at once scribbled back: "If the conversion of the six is to be life from the dead to the six hundred, what then?"[7]

"The great event of Israel's return to God in Christ, and His to Israel," said Bishop Handley C. G. Moule, honorary chaplain to the queen of England from 1898 to 1901, "will be the signal and the means of a vast rise of spiritual life in the universal church, and of an unexampled ingathering of regenerate souls from the world."[8]

43

Andrew Bonar (nineteenth century) believed Israel to be the "everlasting nation" that is to be life from the dead to all nations.[9] Count Zinzendorf, the spiritual leader of the Moravians in the eighteenth century, looked for wholesale conversion of many tribal peoples only after the Jewish people returned to the Lord.[10]

The great English expositor C. H. Spurgeon wrote: "I think we do not attach enough importance to the restoration of the Jews. . . . But certainly, if there is anything promised in the Bible, it is this. . . . The day shall yet come when the Jews, who were the first apostles to the Gentiles, the first missionaries to us who were afar off, shall be gathered in again. Until that shall be, the fullness of the church's glory can never come. Matchless benefits to the world are bound up with the restoration of Israel, their gathering shall be as life from the dead."[11]

These and other men and women of former generations understood Romans 11 to be pointing to a time when the nation of Israel would be reestablished and great numbers of Jewish people would begin to accept the Lord, while at the same time a vast revival would sweep across the whole world.

They were seeing in the Spirit what today is being manifested in the earth.

The Jewish Homecoming and World Revival

Jewish people began returning to Israel in greater numbers in the nineteenth century and are still immigrating by the tens of thousands annually. The number of Messianic Jewish believers and congregations is increasing rapidly. And the world is experiencing the greatest spiritual awakening in history. According to Paul (and those biblical students of former generations), these facts are inextricably bound to each other: Israel's homecoming—both physical and spiritual—and world revival. Watch how these events merge.

Seventy percent of all those who have ever come to faith in Jesus have come since the first Zionist conference in Basel, Switzerland, in 1897. At the birth of Zionism—the movement that heralds the right of the Jewish people to the Land—the ratio of believers to unbelievers was 1 to 27; today that number is 1 to 5.

Seventy percent of those who have come to faith since the birth of Zionism, or over 50 percent of those who have ever come to faith, have come since the founding of the State of Israel in 1948. According to Ralph Winter and the Center for World Missions in Pasadena, California, the number of evangelical believers is growing 3.5 times faster than the population of the world.

Seventy percent of all who have ever come to faith in Jesus have come since the birth of Zionism. Seventy percent of those have come since the birth of the nation of Israel.

While there were only 3 percent of Africans who called themselves Christian at the time of Zionism's inception, today over 50 percent identify with the Christian faith. South Korea was only 1 percent Christian in 1897, but it is now nearing 40 percent. The largest church in the world is the Full Gospel Church in Seoul, Korea, with over 700,000 members.

In India there are now 103 million believers, with a new church being birthed every seven minutes among the Hindus.

More Muslims have come to believe in Jesus since 1980 than in all the previous 1,000 years. Statistics from the Lausanne Task Force on Evangelism state that while Islam continues to grow at a 3.2 percent annual rate, faith in Jesus is increasing worldwide at a rate of 6.9 percent annually.

In Indonesia an estimated 20 percent of the population is now Christian.

Consider also the birth of modern Pentecostalism (the rediscovery of the Spirit's work) and the birth of Zionism—the move to reestablish the State of Israel—both happening around the turn of the nineteenth century.

The Latter Rain Revival, the great healing ministry that swept through the world fifty years ago, also occurred almost simultaneously with the birth of the State of Israel in 1948.

The Six-Day War of 1967, in which Israel took possession of Jerusalem, is strangely the same year as the beginning of the Jesus Movement, through which so many Jewish young people began to believe that Jesus/Yeshua is the Messiah of Israel. I have a copy of the June 1971 *Time* magazine. Three times, 1967 is called the beginning of both the Jesus Movement and the charismatic movement, a movement that attracted "Roman Catholics and Jews, Protestants of every persuasion and many with no religion at all."[12] Remember that 1967 is also the year in which Israel reclaimed Jerusalem as their capital city. No coincidence!

This great world movement is not sparked by one mission organization alone; it is the work of the united people of God. The psalmist spoke of blessing that would come when the Lord's family "live together in unity" (Psalm 133:1). Jesus Himself prayed for unity among believers so that the watching world might believe (see John 17:21–23). The promise of the psalmist and the prayer of Jesus are gradually coming to fruition. This awakening of the nations is happening through the united efforts of people from most of the major Christian groups.

The AD 2000 movement to evangelize every nation and every unreached people group of the world involved people of every denomination. It was accompanied by the greatest prayer effort ever launched in history. An estimated 30 million were involved in prayer movements, often united through the aid of the Internet and often by praying for the same people groups on the same day.

There continue to be prayer mountains and prayer centers, not only in Korea and Kansas City, but in many major cities of the world. Our own Middle Tennessee prayer retreat center will soon be another location for world intercessors and worshipers to join together, agreeing with heaven for this advancing revival. "Thy kingdom come! Thy will be done on earth as it is in heaven!"

Bill Bright of Campus Crusade believed the Lord showed him that two million people fasting for forty days would usher in the world harvest.[13] Stadiums filling with worshipers, cell groups and house churches forming, global reconciliation movements flourishing, denominational mission agencies and parachurch ministries cooperating for the task! In spite of our weaknesses, there is greater worldwide togetherness and passion for the lost than at any time in history.

That this unprecedented growth parallels Israel's physical restoration to the Land and a firstfruits harvest of Jewish believers in Jesus would not have surprised some of these saints of the past. Life from the dead for millions! Greater riches for the whole world! Just as Leighton, Owen, M'Cheyne, Simeon, Moule, Bonar and others thought it would be. Just as the apostle Paul knew it would be!

Cycle of Revival

My friend and colleague, Tod McDowell, began calling all of this "God's cycle of revival."

Paul tells the Romans, "If their [Jewish] transgression means riches for the world . . . and their [Jewish] loss means riches for the Gentiles, how much greater riches [for the whole world, the nations, everyone], will their fullness bring! . . . If their [Jewish] rejection is the reconciliation of the world [the nations], what will their acceptance be [Jewish people coming to faith], but life from the dead?" (11:12, 15).

Phase 1: Jewish people coming to faith releases "greater riches . . . life from the dead" to the nations. The Jewish people have come into their destiny of becoming a "light for the Gentiles" (Isaiah 42:6; 49:6).

But there is more.

Paul continues, "Just as you [Gentiles, non-Jews] who were at one time disobedient to God have now received mercy as a result

47

of their [Jewish] disobedience, so they too have now become disobedient in order that they too may now receive mercy as a result of God's mercy to you" (Romans 11:30–31).

Phase 2: When believers from the nations begin showing genuine unconditional mercy and love to the Jewish people, more of them will come to faith in their Messiah, coming into their fullness and becoming a light to the nations.

Phase 3: When Jewish people come to faith and enter into their destiny, this will release greater riches, life from the dead to the nations and the cycle is complete.

Paul concludes his thoughts with a challenge to his Gentile readers: "In view of God's mercy [this mercy shown to you Gentiles] . . . offer your bodies as living sacrifices" (12:1).

In other words, "Because you have received Israel's Messiah when they, as a nation, did not, your role now is to show them mercy because you have received the blessings that were originally intended for them . . . as well as for you."

Unfortunately, this kind of mercy has not often been extended through all the generations and centuries . . . until our day! Thanks be to God, this mutual love, this beneficial love between Jew and Gentile, is making some strides forward in our time.

Signs and Wonders

As in the first century, much of the harvest of the twentieth and twenty-first centuries has come as a result of the sovereign intervention of the Lord through signs, healings, angelic visitations and other miracles. Christian bookstores are filled with books and magazines verifying these phenomena.

A Baptist missionary in Yemen tells of tribal Muslims who had dreams about the Son of God and came to the capital city to find Christians who could explain more about this Man "who calls Himself Jesus Christ."[14]

In India a blind woman named Madu had heard of the *Jesus* film. From her scant knowledge of the Scriptures, Madu remembered a blind man named Bartimaeus who had called out for mercy and was healed. *Does the God of Jesus truly work miracles?* she wondered. As she drifted off to sleep, she murmured, "I am a poor woman, and I need help, too."

Early the next morning her family awakened to Madu's screams. Rushing to her bedside, they found her rejoicing. "I can see! I can see!" she cried. Word of this Jesus who could heal reached the surrounding villages and many responded in faith.[15]

In 1983, in a North African village located about 125 miles from Algiers, the Lord began to move from house to house, communicating through visions, dreams and angelic visitations. He did not rest until every member of this Muslim community had been introduced to Him. At daybreak the villagers began to tell their stories. In the days and weeks that followed, 400 to 450 of the villagers became believers in Jesus as the Messiah. As missionaries began to research the history of the village, they found that over 500 years earlier, a Spanish missionary from Majorca had been stoned to death on this very site. That missionary, Raymond Lull, had written that Islamic strongholds are best conquered "by love and prayers, and the pouring out of tears and blood."[16]

Missionaries arriving among the Fali in North Africa were greeted with the question, "Are you the messengers sent to tell us about the arrival of God's Son?"[17] For hundreds of years this people had believed that one day God would have a Son and would send messengers to tell them about the event. When they received the message, they would know that the end of the world was near.

Samaa Habib, a former Muslim from one of the USSR countries, tells her own story of coming to faith in Jesus at a young age after feeling the love of the Jesus-followers.[18] Though persecuted for her faith, actually *killed* in a bomb explosion during one of their worship gatherings, she had an encounter with Jesus, who gave her the opportunity to come back to witness to her family. Today, this beautiful young woman, whose skin is amazingly restored without scars, has had the delight of welcoming her parents and most of her siblings as fellow believers.

Tod and I have experienced firsthand the amazing revival in Mozambique. We have ministered side by side with Heidi Baker, who with her husband, Rolland, founded Iris Global Network. We have prayed and seen blind eyes open, the deaf-mute speak, the lame walk. We were in a Muslim village and heard the chief of the village invite believers in Jesus to minister among them, assuring us, "We have no problem with people believing in Jesus." Heidi told of all the blind people for whom she prayed before one eye was opened. And then one day, saturated with God-compassion, she saw a little grandmother who did not even have eyes in the sockets where they were supposed to have been. Heidi embraced her and cried out, "Oh, Jesus!" only to witness eyes forming and the woman beginning to see. Iris Ministries has begun thousands of churches throughout Mozambique and other surrounding nations.

Life from the dead! Greater riches! Jesus said, "This gospel of the kingdom will be preached in the whole world as a testimony to all nations" (Matthew 24:14).

If Robert Leighton, John Owen and the others were correct in their understanding of Romans 11:12 and 15—and according to the evidence of our time, they were—then the greatest world revival among both Jews and Gentiles is just ahead. This grand world awakening has only just begun. The people chosen to bring light to the whole world will fulfill its destiny. This nation of priests, who have blessed others, will yet enter into its greatest time of blessing.

Remarks from David McQueen,
pastor, Beltway Park Baptist Church, Abilene, Texas

For much of my Christian life, I was a functional replacement theologian—I believed the Church had utterly replaced

Israel, and all the promises of God directed to the Jewish people now applied only to the Church. In essence, God was finished with the Jewish people except for a handful who had come to faith in their Messiah. Interestingly, I had never heard anyone teach this explicitly. It was assumed so deeply, there was no need to teach it.

In the year 2000, after being called to a pastorate in Abilene, Texas, I called Don Finto, asking to travel with him, desiring as a young pastor to gain wisdom from his years of pastoral leadership. He informed me that he was soon to be going to the annual meeting of the Messianic Jewish Alliance of America (MJAA) meeting in Pennsylvania, and that I was free to join him. Although I had no information about MJAA, I decided to make the trip with Don, not then understanding his heart for Israel and the Jewish people.

When I arrived at Don's home, ready to accompany him on the trip, he handed me a manuscript copy of *Your People Shall Be My People*. The book was soon to be released by Gospel Light Regal. Don suggested that I read some of the book so that I would know more about the groups we would meet at the conference. Ironically, I was young and brash enough (which sounds kinder than arrogant) to believe that Dr. Finto wanted my critique and input on his book.

On the flight to Pennsylvania, I began reading, making editorial marks in the margins (though I myself had never written anything). When Don referenced Romans 11:12, I was stunned and perplexed. How could this man have so utterly misquoted Scripture? I had read Romans dozens of times, often in the original Greek. I knew the letter well (so I thought), and was confident that this verse was not a part of Paul's letter.

I stood up to get my Bible out of the overhead bin so that I could show Don his error. He asked what I was doing, and I told him I thought he had misquoted Paul. He smiled

51

knowingly, assuring me that the manuscript had been well edited.

I opened my Bible to Romans 11 and began to read. It was as if I had never seen this passage before. I knew immediately that I was in a divine moment of revelation as the Father was inviting me to join in with His purposes for the Jewish people and their connection to world revival as their eyes are opening to their Messiah.

Don and I continued on our journey to the MJAA conference, where we spent several days with Jewish believers and with their covenant Gentile partners. I returned to Abilene, shared my newfound revelation with our leadership, began to take groups of leaders to Israel and have become an avid advocate for this newly resurrected community of Jewish believers in Jesus.

Israel—A Nation of Priests

You will be for me a kingdom of priests and a holy nation.

Exodus 19:6

Martha and I had heard of Corrie ten Boom and had read of this Dutch woman's determination to give shelter to Jewish people during the Nazi reign of terror in Europe. When the movie of Corrie's life story, *The Hiding Place,* came to the theaters, we went to see it. When the film ended, we were so overwhelmed with emotion that we could scarcely leave our seats. We remained silent as we left the theater and drove home. Once there, we even went into separate rooms and wept until we could regain sufficient composure to process what had happened to us.

These were God's people, the closest blood relatives of our Lord. What a miracle that any of them were still alive! And to have maintained their national identity through two thousand years without a homeland? Impossible! Except that God had miraculously kept them.

In a largely anti-Semitic world just fifty years ago, the United Nations had voted by a two-thirds majority to appropriate her ancient homeland for the reestablishment of the modern State of Israel. It could not have happened a year earlier or a year later. God chose a small window of time for the words of the prophets to find their fulfillment.

One thing distinguishes this people from all other families on earth: God chose them as a nation of priests for the world. "Although the whole earth is mine, you will be for me a kingdom of priests and a holy nation," He told Moses as He led the Israelites through the desert out of Egyptian bondage (Exodus 19:5–6). Now Israel was to represent God to the nations until "all the ends of the earth will see the salvation of our God" (Isaiah 52:10).

God's initial call and promise to Abraham included not only the Land—"The whole land of Canaan, where you are now an alien, I will give as an everlasting possession to you and your descendants after you" (Genesis 17:8)—but also that "all peoples on earth will be blessed through you" (12:3).

"Through your offspring all nations on earth will be blessed" was God's reaffirmation to Isaac (26:4).

And to Jacob? The Lord appeared to him during his flight from Esau, and assured him that he was the carrier of the Abrahamic promise: "I am the LORD, the God of your father Abraham and the God of Isaac. I will give you and your descendants the land on which you are lying. . . . All peoples on earth will be blessed through you and your offspring" (28:13–14).

The prophets understood this prophetic priestly call on the nation of Israel. "Nations will come to your light and kings to the brightness of your dawn," proclaimed Isaiah (60:3). "I will keep you and will make you to be a covenant for the people and a light for the Gentiles . . . that you may bring my salvation to the ends of the earth" (42:6; 49:6).

When the aged Simeon saw Jesus with His parents on the day of His infant consecration, the old man's words rang with the spirit of the prophets: "Sovereign Lord, as you have promised, you now dismiss your servant in peace. For my eyes have seen your salvation, which you have prepared in the sight of all people, *a light for revelation to the Gentiles* and for glory to your people Israel" (Luke 2:29–32, emphasis mine).

But it would not be easy to keep this fledgling people free from idolatry. Even while Moses was receiving God's instructions for them, they reverted to pagan practices when he stayed too long on the mountain. The people wanted gods like those they had known in Egypt—gods they could see and touch. Aaron tried a compromise. He took their gold, fashioned it into a golden calf and said, "Tomorrow there will be a festival to the LORD" (Exodus 32:5). In other words, "Let us worship God in the form of this golden calf!" It didn't work. The Lord would not accept the compromise. Three thousand Israelites died in one day (see Exodus 32:1–5, 28). An interesting little aside is that centuries later, when Israel's promised Messiah came and redemption was brought in His name, three thousand *were saved* in one day (see Acts 2:41).

When Moses finally came down the mountain with the commandments of God, the first three commandments had to do with Israel's faithfulness to the Lord: "You shall have no other gods before me. You shall not make for yourself an idol. . . . You shall not misuse the name of the LORD your God" (Exodus 20:3–4, 7).

This essential faithfulness to the one true God became the cornerstone of Jewish faith and is still expressed twice daily by observant Jews, and weekly in every synagogue of the world in the words of the *Shema*: "Hear, O Israel: The LORD our God, the LORD is one" (Deuteronomy 6:4).

Israel was to remain a separated nation. For this reason, intermarriage was forbidden. Even Solomon, with all his wisdom, was ensnared by his foreign wives with their foreign gods. It was idolatry that brought about the ultimate demise of both the northern and southern kingdoms.

Speaking prophetically for YHWH, this God whose name is so sacred that most Jewish people would never attempt to speak it, Isaiah lamented, "I reared children and brought them up, but they have rebelled against me" (1:2). This is God, mourning His lost and wayward children!

It was this uniqueness of the one true God—His insistence upon their faithfulness to Him alone—that was Israel's challenge.

The Canaanites, the Egyptians, the Greeks and the Romans did not object to Israel's God as long as He was only one of many. But God had clearly stated, "No other gods." Israel was set apart to worship Him alone, to keep faith alive in Him.

> *The nations of the world have worshiped their many gods, but only Israel and religious faith born out of Jewish roots have maintained that "the LORD our God, the LORD is one."*

The nations of the world have worshiped their many gods, but only Israel and religious faith born out of Jewish roots have maintained that "the LORD our God, the LORD is one."

A God Who Rests

The fourth commandment that Moses brought from his mountain encounter with the Lord set aside one specific day each week for rest:

> Remember the Sabbath day by keeping it holy. Six days you shall labor and do all your work, but the seventh day is a Sabbath to the LORD your God. . . . For in six days the LORD made the heavens and the earth . . . but he rested on the seventh day.
>
> Exodus 20:8–11

What a novel idea! A God who encouraged rest. A God who did not enslave His people. No nation had ever known such a God.

By observing the weekly Sabbath, the Jewish family would forever be declaring the virtues of a God who provides for His people. Economics were not to be the determining factor of their lives. If they would live in obedience to His commands, He would provide enough in six days so they could rest on the seventh.

Israel's God affirmed this commitment to His Word for forty years in the desert. Each day the people were to gather manna for one day, but on the sixth day they were to collect enough for two days; there was to be no harvest on the Sabbath. Some tried hoarding manna; others paid no attention to the command of the Lord and did not gather any for the Sabbath. Both groups were forcefully shown that God would be faithful to His Word (see Exodus 16:4, 14–20).

This Sabbath rest was not only for the Israelites but was also to extend even to servants and animals. And there was more. Every seventh year the *land* was to rest. The people were to trust in God's provision for that sabbatical year. "Whatever the land yields during the sabbath year will be food for you," the Lord had told Moses (Leviticus 25:6). Israel was practicing what farmers were later to learn—that the nutrients of the soil can be replenished by allowing the land to lie fallow for a year.

A God Who Protects

No government of the world could compete with the government of Israel. Hers was a monarchy ruled by God Himself. When compared to the legal systems of the world at that time, this system was astonishingly superior in kindness and mercy.

The remainder of the Ten Commandments forms the bedrock for interpersonal relations in the family and in the community: "Honor your father and your mother. . . . You shall not murder. . . . You shall not commit adultery. . . . You shall not steal. . . . You shall not give false testimony. . . . You shall not covet" (Exodus 20:12–17).

These commandments, if obeyed, would revolutionize society. There would be no need for courts or prisons, no need for police or security systems. Parents would remain together and both children and the elderly would be cherished members of the family.

Additional laws upheld high standards of morality and personal righteousness. Provisions were made for orphans and widows, and there were guidelines to be followed when accidents occurred. No nation had ever been given such humane and compassionate laws. Yet knowing that the people would not follow these laws, God also allowed for their weaknesses and the age in which they lived, providing rules for indentured servants and slaves and rules for divorce and polygamy. In the times when Israel followed the laws most closely, national leaders came from great distances to observe (see 1 Kings 10:24).

In more modern times, Israel has had amazing health standards above those of her day. For example, in 1847, a Viennese physician, Dr. Ignaz Semmelweis, saw a dramatic reduction in the death rate of his patients when he began to wash his hands after examining diseased patients or after performing autopsies on those who had died. When he attempted to institute this practice among other doctors in his obstetrical ward, he was dismissed from the hospital. After several months, he was able to obtain a position in a hospital in Budapest. There, too, the mortality rate of pregnant women was remarkably reduced when Dr. Semmelweis made these unusual demands of his staff.[1] His secret? The good doctor was only applying the principles God had given Moses many centuries earlier (see Numbers 19:11–14).

In the early 1900s, Dr. Hiram N. Wineberg observed that cervical cancer was nonexistent in his Jewish patients. Studies conducted in 1949, at New York's Bellevue Hospital, at Mayo Clinic and in Boston in 1954 further substantiated the claim that wives of circumcised males had fewer cases of cancer than those whose mates were uncircumcised.[2] Almost four millennia earlier, God had given Israel a covenant sign that protected their women from disease.

God said to Abraham, "For the generations to come every male among you who is eight days old must be circumcised" (Genesis 17:12). Recent research has found that a newborn infant has a peculiar susceptibility to bleeding between the second and fifth days of life. Vitamin K, the substance that aids in clotting, is not adequately formed in the child's system until the seventh day.[3] What a remarkable "coincidence"!

Leviticus 3:17 records the admonition, "You must not eat any fat." This dictate was issued to Israel long before the world knew anything about cholesterol. Fidelity in marriage was practiced without knowing anything about venereal disease. In short, the Lord told Moses, "If you listen carefully to the voice of the LORD your God and do what is right in his eyes, if you pay attention to his commands and keep all his decrees, I will not bring on you any of the diseases I brought on the Egyptians, for I am the LORD, who heals you" (Exodus 15:26). None of these diseases! What a promise!

Through the centuries, God has supernaturally protected His people Israel, not from disease alone, but from her enemies. As a priestly nation, she would perpetually live in a hostile environment. To assure Abraham of continued protection, the Lord spoke in a vision, saying, "Do not be afraid, Abram. I am your shield" (Genesis 15:1).

> *God has supernaturally protected His people Israel during the plots of the Hamans and the Hitlers throughout the centuries.*

He shielded Israel from annihilation and assimilation during her four hundred years in Egypt and brought her back to the Land. He kept her during the plots of the Hamans and the Hitlers throughout the centuries of persecution and reestablished her.

Remembrance and Proclamation in the Feasts

To encourage His people and to proclaim to the world both His faithfulness and the coming righteous King, God ordered the observance of certain annual festivals. Israel, as priests for the world, was to instruct the nations through the story of redemption made clear in the enactment of their biblical feasts.

Pesach (Passover) recalled Israel's deliverance from tyranny and was an annual reminder of the horrors of oppression and the joys of freedom. The original Passover observed in Egypt—in which the blood of a lamb was sprinkled on the doorposts of Jewish homes so that death could "pass over" and spare the firstborn sons—pointed to the Deliverer, whose blood would carry the sins of the people and through whom a whole nation of "firstborn" would be brought forth (see Hebrews 12:23).

John the Baptist called Jesus "the Lamb of God, who takes away the sin of the world" (John 1:29). The celebration of Passover now becomes not only a remembrance of the exodus from Egypt but also a celebration of the Lamb who has come and foreshadows the ultimate Passover/exodus of worldwide proportions described in John's Revelation when only those who have appropriated the blood will be delivered (see 12:11).

The *Hag HaMatzah* (Feast of Unleavened Bread) begins at Passover and lasts for seven days. Jesus compared Himself to the manna that fell in the wilderness, calling Himself "the living bread that came down from heaven. If anyone eats of this bread, he will live forever" (John 6:51, see also verses 41, 50, 58). Piercing, bruising, stripes—all descriptive of *Matzah* and of Jesus—are mentioned by both Isaiah (53:5, 10 NKJV) and Peter (1 Peter 2:24). During the seven days of this feast, nothing with leaven is to be eaten. The leaven—the yeast that puffs up the bread—is a symbol of sin that must be eradicated and is a reminder of the haste with which the children of Israel had to leave Egypt. But the further lesson here is that we are all to remain in a state of preparedness as we anticipate our departure.

The Feast of *Bikkurim* (firstfruits) is, significantly, on the third day after Passover. One sheaf of grain was to be waved before the Lord in proclamation of other fruit to come. Paul tells the Corinthians that Jesus, raised from the dead, is "the firstfruits of those who have fallen asleep" (1 Corinthians 15:20). Jesus' resurrection is the sheaf being waved before a watching world that speaks of resurrections to come.

Shavuot, or Pentecost (Feast of Weeks, also known as the Feast of Harvest), rejoices in God's providential care. The first *Shavuot* occurred at the time of the giving of the Law on Mount Sinai. That Law was the precursor of another law and another harvest—the law written not on tablets of stone but on the tablets of the human heart (see Jeremiah 31:33). It was Pentecost morning, fifty days after Jesus' crucifixion, when the breath of the Spirit blew through Jerusalem, inscribing this new law of love—law of life—on the hearts of the waiting disciples (see Acts 2:1–4; Romans 8:1–2).

The fall feasts begin with *Yom Teruach* (Day of Blowing—Feast of Trumpets), commonly referred to as *Rosh Hashanah* (literally meaning "head of the year"). The *shofar* (trumpet) is blown to usher in the beginning of the civil year and to begin the Ten Days of Awe from *Rosh Hashanah* to *Yom Kippur* (Day of Atonement). This is a time of introspection and self-examination as we anticipate the trumpet sounds that will announce the Lord's arrival (see 1 Corinthians 15:52; 1 Thessalonians 4:16–17; Revelation 10:7; 11:15).

Yom Kippur illustrates, like no other singular day in Israel's calendar, man's sinfulness and the need for pardon. Early on this "atonement day," Israel would come to the priests, confessing their sins; the priests would confess to the high priest. Through the confession of the people and the priests, a goat symbolically bore the sins of the nations and was killed in place of the people. The high priest then slaughtered the goat for the sin offering (see Leviticus 16:15) and entered the holy of holies, "never without blood, which he offered for himself and for the sins the people had committed" (Hebrews 9:7).

This whole process of confessing sins was repeated with a second goat. The high priest was to "lay both hands on the head of the live goat and confess over it all the wickedness and rebellion of the Israelites—all their sins—and put them on the goat's head" (Leviticus 16:21), at which point the goat was released into the desert.

Interesting! An animal had just been sacrificed for the sins of the people, and yet now the one bearing the "sins" was sent into the wilderness. How could this be? The writer of Hebrews knew the truth behind the symbolism. He called these offerings "an annual reminder of sins" and assures us that "it is impossible for the blood of bulls and goats to take away sins" (10:3–4).

Thousands of animals were slaughtered each year, each one a prophecy of the Lamb that was to come. Only He—this one Man, this sinless Man—could carry the human burden and take upon Himself the sins of all of Adam's family, freeing all who would accept His payment (see Isaiah 53:5, 10). This man was Yeshua, Jesus the Christ, the Messiah.

In His last supper with His disciples at Passover, Jesus, our Passover "Lamb" (our "Atonement Goat," though this is a shocking thought!) referred to the bread and wine as His own body and blood. "This is my body given for you. . . . This cup is the new covenant in my blood, which is poured out for you" (Luke 22:19–20).

For centuries now, when believers observe the Supper of the Lord, holding in their hands the elements—simple bread and wine—scenes of that last supper with Jesus flash before their eyes. For the discerning heart, every loaf of bread, every bottle of wine becomes a visible reminder of the body of Yeshua, of His blood that has saved us.

Five days after Yom Kippur is *Sukkoth,* the Feast of Tabernacles (or Booths), the last of Israel's major feasts (the other two are Passover and Pentecost), which every Jewish male was required to attend. This was the time of the final ingathering of the harvest, anticipating the immense harvest of souls prior to Yeshua's return. Through this annual feast, the people of God were made aware of their years of wandering and of the temporary nature of their earthly housing as, for eight days each year, the faithful dwell in a *sukkah* (booth). The apostle tells us that Jesus "dwelt [or tabernacled] among us" (John 1:14 KJV).[4] Our dwelling is also temporary. The greatest "housing"—many mansions—lies ahead!

According to the Jerusalem apostolic ruling (see Acts 15:1–35), Gentiles were not given the requirement to observe these feasts, yet the Hebrew Scriptures (Old Testament) were the only Scriptures available to these Gentile Jesus-followers. The apostolic writings (New Testament) were not completed until at least the latter part of the first century and were not gathered together in one unit until decades later. We know from Paul's letter to Corinth, that, though they may not have been given the command, many of the Gentile believers were feast-observers. "For Christ, our Passover lamb, has been sacrificed. Therefore let us keep the Festival, not with the old yeast, the yeast of malice and wickedness, but with bread without yeast, the bread of sincerity and truth," Paul admonished the believers in Corinth (1 Corinthians 5:7–8).

These are, after all, not Jewish feasts, but "the LORD's appointed feasts" (Leviticus 23:4), and continue to have prophetic significance for all believers—something to which many of us from the nations can attest. For this reason, Passover meals, Pentecost celebrations, Feast of Tabernacles gatherings, even Sabbath observances are making their reentrance into the communities of Gentile believers. More and more of us desire to reclaim our lost heritage, even though we may still use our traditional holidays for beckoning people to follow Jesus.

Blessing to the Nations

The Lord told Abraham that the nations of the earth would be blessed through his descendants. This has been fulfilled in amazing ways. The Jewish people have blessed the world in total disproportion to their number. The Jewish world population, though only one-fourth of 1 percent, has produced 15 percent of the Nobel Prize winners since the inception of that award in 1899.[5] Even that number is astonishing in view of the millions of Jewish people who have been driven from their homes and often to their deaths.

Their contributions to the world have truly been a blessing to all the earth. In his book *What the Church Owes the Jew*, Leslie Flynn wrote,

> If an anti-Semite decided to boycott all the tests and cures discovered by the Jews, he would certainly open himself to a host of serious diseases. Besides refusing Jonas Salk's polio vaccine, he would also decline the polio pill by Dr. Albert Sabin; the test to fight diphtheria invented by Bela Schick; the diet regime of Joseph Goldberger which has fought pellagra to a standstill; blood transfusions made possible by the work of Dr. E. J. Cohen of Harvard . . . the Wasserman test for syphilis; the vaccine for hepatitis discovered by Baruch Blumberg; streptomycin discovered by Dr. Selman Abraham Waxman as an antibiotic . . . ; chlorohydrate for convulsions discovered by Dr. J. Von Liebig; and vitamins discovered by Casimir Funk.
>
> U.S. Jews are twice as likely to go to college as Gentiles, are five times more likely to be admitted to an Ivy League school, and are over-represented in the fields of medicine, science, law, and dentistry.[6]

The world of music, too, would be greatly diminished without its Jewish composers, conductors, pianists, violinists and opera singers. Eugene Ormandy, James Levine, Arthur Fiedler, Isaac Stern, Jascha Heifetz, Yehudi Menuhin, Jerome Kern, Irving Berlin, Oscar Hammerstein, George Gershwin, Artur Rubenstein, Paul Simon and Richard Rodgers are household names.

Similar lists can be compiled in the areas of philosophy, journalism, philanthropy, politics and sports.

John Adams wrote in a letter to F. A. Van der Kemp,

I will insist that the Hebrews have done more to civilize men than any other nation. . . . If I were an atheist . . . I should believe that chance had ordered the Jews to preserve and to propagate to all mankind the doctrine of a supreme, intelligent, wise, almighty sovereign of the universe, which I believe to be the great essential principle of all morality, and consequently, of all civilization.[7]

When Frederick the Great asked his chaplain for one reason to believe in God, the chaplain is supposed to have said, "The amazing Jew, your majesty."

Having so often been beaten down, driven from their homes, their wealth confiscated and their lives endangered, this Jacob family has consistently been elevated to positions of leadership in the nations where they have been dispersed. Threatened repeatedly with extermination, they have risen to bless the very people who have oppressed them. In all their suffering, their priestly role continues.

Remarks from Avner Boskey, Final Frontier Ministry, Omer, Israel

God's calling on the Jewish people to be priests to the nations is one of the closely guarded secrets of Scripture. Though it is taught in plain view, somehow this and other gifts and callings given to and through the Jewish people have been swept under the theological carpet throughout much of church history.

The amazing calling in Isaiah 49:5–6—for the descendants of Jacob to become a light to the nations and a servant people (imitating Yeshua, our Servant King)—is an amazing privilege to which the Jewish prophets and apostles have contributed much. The future aspect of this calling can be seen in such passages as Isaiah 60:1–3 and Zechariah 8:22–23, as well as in Acts 13:22 and Romans 11:12, 15.

When God's light shines from and through Israel in days soon to come, the whole world will "get it"—they will embrace the Jewish Messiah who sits enthroned in a Jewish land and Jewish city, surrounded by His own brothers after the flesh. His calendar (see Leviticus 23:1–2) will become the world's calendar, and His feasts will be celebrated by the nations of the world and not only by the Jewish people!

In that day, God's sovereign guiding hand will be celebrated, as revealed through the feasts, the agricultural cycle of the Promised Land, in the history past of Israel and of the prophetic history future of the Jewish people as the capital of the Messianic kingdom.

As Messianic Jewish believers, we try to keep the centrality of Yeshua and the New Covenant as the main focus of our celebrations and memorial days. We remember that Pentecost marks the breaking in of the New Covenant and that the Feast of Trumpets, God's feast in the seventh month of the biblical year, is fast approaching in the Spirit as God calls His people home to Himself and to His Land.

4

The Targeted Annihilation

> The dragon stood in front of the woman who was about to
> give birth, so that he might devour her child the moment it
> was born.
>
> Revelation 12:4

I will never forget the day I heard Marty Waldman tell what it was like to grow up as the son of Holocaust survivors. Marty's parents had escaped from a Polish labor camp just as World War II was ending. They went first to Germany, then to Austria, before securing passage to the United States, where Marty was born.

Marty was standing in front of me. Behind me sat Rudi Pinke, a German pastor to whom God has given a Jewish heart. Rudi carries the shame of a humbled nation and looks for every opportunity to love his Jewish brothers and sisters.

As Marty described the weight of the grief that still affects his family, he spoke in a voice choked with tears, "I know I need to go back to Poland someday . . . but I have not yet been able to do that."

Upon hearing these words, Rudi sprang from his seat, almost knocking people over in his eagerness to reach Marty. Taking the man in his arms, he said repeatedly, "I'll go with you, Marty! I'll go with you. We'll go together!" They stood there, locked in an embrace of love—the son of a Jew and the son of a German—a preview of greater days to come.[1]

I have had my own God encounters with Jewish people. One of them, Eitan Shishkoff, was a hippie farmer in the mountains of New Mexico when he met Yeshua. He explained to me what it was like growing up in an assimilated home in Southern California. He had become disillusioned with life and wanted reality. God was distant. He needed something tangible. So he gave himself to the soil and to the elements and found relative peace in his soul.

That all changed in one day. Eitan's peaceful community was shattered when a friend was murdered. There was no place to go with his grief. Soon after, two "Jesus people" showed up at Eitan's remote farm, describing the Messiah and His mission of redeeming humanity. While these young, untrained witnesses were speaking, Eitan had a vision of the Jewish Messiah, Jesus, hanging from the cross, eyes blazing like laser beams that pierced Eitan's own heart. It was an experience from which he would never recover.

As Eitan shared his story, the words of the prophets were pounding in my chest—words spoken to Jews: "Then you will know that I am the LORD" (Ezekiel 36:11). Again I was seeing prophecy fulfilled before my eyes.

Eitan and I became covenant friends that day—this West Texas farm boy and the California Jew—our hearts inextricably bound for eternity.[2]

"I Will Stand with You!"

Not all relationships are easy to penetrate. The wound in the Jewish heart is deep, and sometimes it takes years and many close, trusted partners before that wound is healed.

Not all that long ago, I was in a room with Jewish and Gentile leaders in the larger body of Jesus-followers. The horror of the Holocaust was being discussed, and one of the Gentile pastors looked over at one of my Jewish friends and remarked almost casually, "Next time we'll stand with you."

Almost reflexively, as if responding from lifelong pain and betrayal, my Jewish friend blurted out, "I don't believe you!" I think he was shocked at his own words, but added, "That has never been the case in history."

I was heavily impacted by the encounter. Somewhere it was stored in the inner recesses of my soul, so that on another occasion, following a showing of films from the Holocaust, I turned to this same Jewish friend and said, under a Holy Spirit anointing and with tears streaming down my cheeks, "I vow to you in the name of Yeshua, that I will stand with you even to death."

His response? "I believe you, Don."

My prayer for all of us is that we establish such deep friendships across these turbulent ancient "racial" lines, so that even among Jewish people who are not believers in Yeshua, we Gentiles will become the Corrie ten Booms and the Oskar Schindlers of our time.

The Plot to Destroy the Seed

Examples of deep brotherhood between Jew and Gentile are the exception rather than the rule. Anti-Semitism is still the longest held and deepest hatred in human history. This animosity had its beginning in the Garden when God promised Eve that one of her descendants would crush the enemy's head (see Genesis 3:15). The weight of this man-hatred later centered in Abraham and his descendants.

God's call to Abraham has been a mixed blessing. Under God's supernatural protection, the Jewish people have survived, but they have had to endure the wrath of the nations. Since the time of

Abraham's call, Satan has targeted this family for extinction. If he could destroy Abraham's descendants, he would thwart the purposes of God in bringing the world's Deliverer through Israel's promised Son.

After Jesus came, Satan continued his assault against the Jewish nation. He knew that the Jewish Messiah would return one day to a reestablished Jewish homeland and to both Jew and Gentile who are ready to receive Him.

In the meantime, the enemy continued to attempt to seduce Israel through idolatry so that she would no longer be able to serve the purposes of God. If that failed, he would assimilate her into the nations so that she would eventually accept their customs, and her witness to the world would be nullified. The evil one has lurked in every dark corner of history to stalk God's chosen people.

The barrenness of Abraham's wife, Sarah, was one of Satan's first attempts to abort the promise. Not believing that God could open Sarah's ninety-year-old womb, Abraham and Sarah interfered with His plan by substituting her handmaiden, Hagar, to guarantee the promised heir. The results of this interference are seen in the ongoing hostility between the sons of Ishmael and the sons of Israel (between Muslims and Jews). But God did not need any help, and He later provided the child through Sarah, just as He said He would (see Genesis 18:14).

That son, Isaac, was forty years old when he married his cousin Rebecca. For the next twenty years, she was barren. But Isaac prayed, the Lord heard and answered and Rebecca gave birth to twins, Esau and Jacob.

From the time God chose Jacob's family as the people of promise, the invisible enemy from the Garden orchestrated many events and circumstances to try to eliminate them. If he could do away with this one family, all the people of the earth would not be blessed through Abraham and his descendants. God's Word would be proven wrong and Adam's children forever separated from Father God.

Already, within Jacob's immediate family, we see the battle lines drawn. Famine came to the land, a famine that could have wiped out the family. But God had sent Joseph to Egypt to prepare a place of refuge for them. The Lord used even the jealousy of Joseph's brothers to His own good purposes. "Do not be distressed and do not be angry with yourselves for selling me here," Joseph told them, "because it was to save lives that God sent me ahead of you . . . to preserve for you a remnant on earth and to save your lives by a great deliverance" (Genesis 45:5, 7).

Things went well with this remnant of God's people as He poured out His blessings on them in the land of Goshen. Ultimately, however, there arose a pharaoh who realized that the Egyptians were becoming dangerously outnumbered. If he could kill all the sons of Israel, the race would soon be assimilated into Egyptian culture and forgotten. This decree appears to have come from the pharaoh, but a more sinister force was at work. Under the Egyptian tyrant's cruel regime, the children of Israel became captives.

In the ensuing years there were other miracles of deliverance—at the Red Sea, in the wilderness, at the crossing of the Jordan, at Jericho and other cities—all reminders of Israel's destiny.

Finally back in her own Land, Israel underwent a four-hundred-year cycle of idolatry and repentance before God chose her second king, David, as the bearer of "the seed." The Messiah was to be a "son of David." But from that day forward, not only the nation of Israel but now, specifically, David's house would become the focal point of Satan's schemes.

God's Promise Is Sure

The nation soon divided into two kingdoms—the majority of the tribes breaking off to form a new nation in the north. Nine dynasties reigned over that nation in the next two centuries. But

71

in the small southern kingdom of Judah, a descendant of David was on the throne. There were many wars and many attempts to destroy David's house, but none of the attempts succeeded. God was watching over His promise.

In one interesting six-year span, it appeared as if the enemy had won. Young King Ahaziah was killed in battle. His mother, Athaliah, daughter of Ahab and Jezebel, known for their idolatry, set out to have all of the king's sons killed and to usurp the throne of Judah. She almost got away with it. Only one-year-old Joash was spared. An aunt hid him for six years. At the age of seven, he was brought out of hiding and declared king of Judah (see 2 Kings 11). Until Joash had sons, all of the promises of God—the promise given to Eve in the Garden, the covenant made with Abraham and renewed with Isaac and Jacob, the vow to David—rested in his young body. If Joash had been killed, God would have been proven fallible. But God was not nervous. He is not only the Maker but the Keeper of Promises.

Nation after nation attacked the Jewish people in the following centuries. Foreign powers ruled in Jerusalem—Babylonia, Persia, Greece and Rome all had their day. At times it appeared that the struggling nation would not survive.

Haman, the fifth-century BC "Hitler" of Persia, planned the strategy for Jewish annihilation in his day. It was a woman, Queen Esther, a young Jewess, who was the salvation of her people. Her story is recorded in the Book of Esther and retold annually in the synagogues of the world at the Feast of Purim.

Two hundred years later, the Greek ruler Antiochus Epiphanes controlled Jerusalem. In his attempts to hellenize the Jews—to assimilate them into Greek culture—he actually offered swine in the Temple, the epitome of desecration. Judas Maccabaeus led the charge against this pagan invasion and brought the worship of God back to Israel.[3] The event is commemorated in the annual Hanukkah celebration, known in the New Testament as the Feast of Dedication (see John 10:22).

All efforts to destroy this family of priests were ultimately exhausted, and God's timing was finally right for the Messiah to be brought forth.

In the Fullness of Time

Four thousand years after Eve heard in the Garden God's promise of a Deliverer . . . two thousand years after God's covenant with Abraham . . . one thousand years after David's lineage had been selected, an angel appeared to a young Jewish girl in Nazareth, and a child was conceived. Both Miriam (Mary's Hebrew name) and Joseph, her betrothed, were, as the prophets had foretold, descendants of Abraham, Isaac, Jacob and David. In due time a son was born.

During Jesus' lifetime, the battle raged on. Again and again, Satan tried to assassinate the King of kings—in the slaughter of the firstborn sons of Bethlehem, at the time of the temptation (similar to the Garden temptation—an attempt to bring this "second Adam" under Satan's dominion) and eventually on the cross.

Pilate, too, had issued empty threats. "Don't you realize I have power either to free you or to crucify you?" he taunted. To which Jesus replied, "You would have no power over me if it were not given to you from above" (John 19:10–11).

Days earlier, Jesus had assured His disciples: "I lay down my life for the sheep. No one takes it from me, but I lay it down of my own accord" (John 10:15, 18).

The devil had used every weapon in his arsenal to prevent Jesus' birth, His fulfilled life and His resurrection—all to no avail. Not only had the Messiah been born, but He also completed the task for which He was destined. He had given His life for the sins of the world. Jesus' death was a voluntary act of submission to the Father's will, prophesied by the ancients: "He was crushed for our iniquities; the punishment that brought us peace was upon him. . . . The LORD has laid on him the iniquity of us all" (Isaiah 53:5–6). Mission accomplished!

Now the strategy had to be changed. Word spread that Jesus' disciples had come and stolen His body from the tomb—that He had not risen from the dead as it was believed (see Matthew 28:12–15). And though He was seen by His friends, by the women at the tomb, by the men on the road to Emmaus and by over five hundred witnesses at one time (see 1 Corinthians 15:6), the attack on the bodily resurrection of Christ still runs hot to this day. Theologians through the centuries have circulated all kinds of theories about the resurrection. The enemy of our souls knows what Paul also knew, that "if Christ has not been raised, your faith is futile; you are still in your sins" (see 1 Corinthians 15:17). What a coup for the devil if that were true!

But Messiah has come. He died and is risen from the dead. He has ascended to heaven. His life has been authenticated through God's sovereign power.

The Controversy Continues

Why now the continuation of anti-Semitism on all fronts? Why would Satan still provoke hatred for the Jews? Why would he now need to annihilate them as a race of people? Why have they been a target for persecution throughout the world in every century?

Because our invisible but powerful opponent knows something that many Christians have not discovered—that the promises of God will not be realized if Satan is successful in destroying Israel. The prophets had spoken of her return to the Land. Isaiah was assured that her eyes would not forever remain closed (see Isaiah 6). Paul was confident that a day would come when "all Israel will be saved" (Romans 11:26). Jesus looked forward to the time when Jews would welcome Him to Jerusalem (see Matthew 23:39). Zechariah saw a period when the Lord would pour out upon Israel a Spirit of grace and supplication, a time when He would reveal Himself to her (see Zechariah 12:10). None of this can come about if Jews cease to exist or even if they lose their identity. No, it is essential to the plans of God that this people and their national identity be protected. As the time for fulfillment approaches, Satan's fury will intensify (see Revelation 12:12).

Remember, Paul assured his Gentile converts that God was not finished with Israel. He warned the Gentiles against arrogance. He reminded them that they were grafted into Israel's olive tree. He spoke of the spiritual sap that comes from Jewish roots. He indicated that the Gentile Church cannot be holy in a complete sense without her Jewish older brother, whose birthright she has usurped. He told the Gentiles that they were to make the Jews jealous through their love and faith (see Romans 11).

Why would Satan still provoke hatred for the Jews? Because he knows something that many Christians have not discovered—that the promises of God will not be realized if Satan is successful in destroying Israel.

And yet the Gentile Church has not only failed to protect the Jews, but she has often participated in and even initiated persecution. Why? The enemy is a deceiver, and the Church has been deceived.

Early in Gentile Church history, its leading scholars began to turn against the Jews. John Chrysostom, in the late third and early fourth century, gave eight "Homilies against the Jews." He assaulted their character as murderous, greedy, immoral, vicious criminals. "As for me I hate the synagogue . . . I hate the Jews."[4]

It was Spanish "Christian" rulers Ferdinand and Isabella who exiled, tortured and killed thousands of Jews during the fifteenth-century Spanish Inquisition.

The great Protestant theologian and reformer Martin Luther became a hater of Jews by the end of his life.

Their synagogues should be set on fire. . . . Their homes should likewise be broken down and destroyed. . . . They should be deprived of their prayer books and Talmuds. . . . Their rabbis must be forbidden under threat of death to teach anymore. . . . Passport and traveling privileges should be absolutely forbidden. . . . Let the young and strong Jews and Jewesses be given the flail, the ax, the hoe, the spade, the distaff, and spindle, and let them earn their bread by the sweat of their noses.[5]

Gerhard Kittel, eminent German New Testament scholar, published a book in 1933 on the "Jewish Question." His counsel? That they should accept discrimination and defamation as their due as second-class citizens whose lot is to wander "restless and homeless on the face of the earth."[6]

The pogroms had their origin in "Christian" lands such as Russia and Poland. The origins of the Holocaust? Christian Austria and Germany, countries whose church ledgers were filled with those who had been properly baptized and confirmed.

The Church has been deceived, serving as a pawn in the hands of her enemy. If only Satan could annihilate the Jews or keep them from the revelation about the Messiah who has already come. What more effective way than to use the very ones claiming to be His followers in achieving that annihilation! Or even assimilation. The plans of God will be delayed as long as the Jews do not "come home."

The prophet Jeremiah said, "I will raise up to David a righteous Branch, a King who will reign wisely and do what is just and right in the land. In his days Judah will be saved and Israel will live in safety" (23:5–6). This prophecy had its partial fulfillment in the first coming of the Messiah. Its final fulfillment is yet to come. Judah has not yet been saved, and Israel does not yet live in safety.

Jesus told the Jewish leaders in Jerusalem that He would return only when they received Him (see Matthew 23:38–39). According to Jesus' words that day, a significant number of Jewish people will be back in the Land and will have accepted Him *before* He returns.

Togetherness in Jesus

Ten days after Jesus' ascension to heaven, the Holy Spirit came upon the gathered disciples in fulfillment of Jesus' promise. Thousands began to believe that day. First, there were three thousand (see Acts 2:41), then five thousand—counting only the men (see Acts 4:4)! Yet another time, Peter told a group of gathered believers, "Repent, then, and turn to God, so that your sins may be wiped out, that times of refreshing may come from the Lord, and that he may send the Christ, who has been appointed for you—even Jesus. He must remain in heaven until the time comes for God to restore everything, as he promised long ago through his holy prophets" (Acts 3:19–21).

The restoration of "everything" the prophets had predicted was still to come. This was a *future* date of which Peter was speaking.

What was promised through the prophets? That Israel would be regathered from all the nations (see Jeremiah 16:14–16); that her eyes would be opened (see Isaiah 35:5; Acts 26:18); that she would come to know the Lord (see Ezekiel 37:12–13); that she would still be a light to the nations (see Isaiah 60:1–3); that the wealth of the nations would be brought to her (see Isaiah 60:5, 11); that Jew and Gentile would dwell together in peace in the Messiah (see Isaiah 66:19–21).

Thank God, we are experiencing in our generation not only the return of Israel to her ancient Land but also the coming together of Jews and former enemies as friends.

Even in the Middle East, Arab and Jewish believers are meeting together to establish relationships. For the past several years, Succat Hallel, a 24/7 worship and prayer ministry in Jerusalem, has sponsored a three-day gathering with Jewish believers, Arab Christians and Muslim-background believers in Jesus. The messages are in Hebrew, Arabic and English with worship in both Hebrew and in Arabic. Participants include not only those from Israel and the Palestinians, but also those from Jordan, Egypt and even Indonesia.

Arab and Jewish youth have washed each other's feet, and have traveled together to Irbil, Iraq, to work among the refugees. They are soon to release their own CD of original worship songs in Hebrew and Arabic.

There could hardly be a greater testimony to the power of Jesus to transform enemies into friends.

Marty and Rudi; Eitan and Don; Jew and Gentile; Israeli believers in Yeshua and Palestinian Arab Christians. Together in Messiah. Gradually, perhaps, but it is happening!

Though targeted for annihilation, God's priestly people still live. Israel's blessing to the nations thrives. The natural descendants of Israel and the grafted implants are a proclamation of God's faithfulness, a strange and wonderful togetherness. Where—and how—did it all begin?

Remarks from Marty Waldman,
Messianic Rabbi, Baruch HaShem, Dallas, Texas

It's the miraculous hand of G-d that any Jews survived Hitler's genocidal attempt to cleanse Europe of its Jewish presence. Six million Jews were murdered in the Holocaust—including most of my family. Only one Waldman survived out of the entire Waldman family—my father, Hershel. His parents (my grandparents), his older brother Moshe, and his two sisters, Hanna and Chaya, along with their spouses and children, were all murdered by Hitler's goons.

My mother's family—the Brombergers—experienced a similar catastrophe, leaving only two girls alive after the Jewish cleansing of Europe. My mother, Lana, and her sister, Ceil, were the only two out of the eight members of their immediate family who survived. Of the three and a half million

Jews who lived in Poland before Hitler's invasion, somewhere between 180,000 and 240,000 lived through it.

My life, too, is a miracle! Just to be alive and carry the message of hope and reconciliation is astounding. Most survivors of the Holocaust had a difficult time reconciling the fact that they had been spared while the rest of their families perished. These survivors flourished, nonetheless, and my parents were among them.

My parents had a choice of emigrating to Israel or to America—the Land of Milk and Honey or the Land of Milk and Money. After all was said and done, they chose the United States, where I was born. Our family was small—my parents, my sister, my aunt, two cousins . . . and me. That was it! Although surviving the Holocaust made life more difficult, our little family prospered.

While in my mid-twenties, I came to believe that Yeshua (Jesus) was/is the true Messiah of Israel. Yeshua changed me forever, filling my heart with His peace. My parents also came to faith in Yeshua before they passed from this earth and, likewise, discovered the peace that had been robbed from them by the horrors of the Holocaust. Thanks be to the G-d of our Fathers Abraham, Isaac and Jacob for His faithfulness to our people.

The Early Jewish "Church"

Salvation is from the Jews.
John 4:22

When Shmuel Suran, a New York Jew, opened to the first page
of the *B'rit Hadashah,* the New Testament, he was not prepared
for what he found.

"The book of the generations of Jesus Christ, son of David,
son of Abraham."

"My God! He was a Jew!" That startling statement would
launch Shmuel on a search for the proof that indeed this Man,
whose name had been used to malign Jews for centuries, was Himself an Israeli-born Jew from Bethlehem, the City of David. Just
as the prophets had prophesied. That He was and is the Messiah
of Israel!

What a strange twist this faith in Yeshua has taken during the
past twenty centuries. The promise was made to Abraham, Isaac
and Jacob, founders of the Jewish family, a promise later renewed

81

to King David, that one of their descendants would reign over the nations forever (see Genesis 28:14; 2 Samuel 7:16). Yeshua fit the prophet's description in every detail and was hailed by thousands of Jews as Messiah. Many of the national leaders rejected Him, of course, but significant numbers of priests and other leaders did receive Him (see John 19:38–39; Acts 6:7).

Every aspect of His life was Jewish to the core: His circumcision, His Torah studies—He baffled the Temple leaders with His knowledge of the Scriptures at age twelve (see Luke 2:47)—His annual pilgrimage to Jerusalem for the feasts, His faithful observance of the Sabbath. In teachings and conversations alike, He constantly cited Moses and the prophets. Even when dying on the cross, He gasped out words from one of David's psalms (compare Matthew 27:46 and Psalm 22:1).

His whole life was spent among the Jews. His closest friends and early followers were all Jewish. As Jonathan Cahn reminded us in a meeting of Jewish believers in Phoenix, "Many of the churches of the world are named after Messianic Jews: Saint Peter, Saint James, Saint John, Saint Paul, Saint Mary, Saint Matthew, Saint Andrews. . . ."

Only on rare occasions did Jesus have an interchange with those not under the covenant, even though it was His full intention that one day the Gospel would go out to the nations. In some of His last remarks to His closest friends, He told them they were to "make disciples of all nations" (Matthew 28:19), "go into all the world" (Mark 16:15), that "repentance and forgiveness of sins will be preached in his [Jesus] name to all nations" (Luke 24:47) and that they would be His witnesses "to the ends of the earth" (Acts 1:8).

His death was not without the involvement of Gentiles—the Roman soldiers, Pilate, Herod. Jesus Himself told His disciples, "The Son of Man will be betrayed to the chief priests and the teachers of the law. They will condemn him to death and will *turn him over to the Gentiles to be mocked and flogged and crucified*" (Matthew 20:18–19, emphasis mine). Though the Jewish people have repeatedly been called the "Christ-killers," it was the Gentiles, not the Jews, who actually committed the murder.

But most of those surrounding the cross were the Jewish people who had watched and followed for the three years of His public ministry.

Resurrection morning at the tomb? Jews, except for the Roman guards who "were so afraid" of the angel that "they shook and became like dead men" (Matthew 28:4). The resurrection appearances during the next forty days? Jews. On the mountain of ascension? Jews again—only Jews. The 120 in the Upper Room waiting for "the gift" (Acts 1:4)? Every one of them a son or daughter of Abraham.

What about Pentecost morning? The recipients of the gift were Jews. And Peter called the prophet Joel and King David as witnesses that Jesus was the manifestation of what these men had seen (see Acts 2:16, 25). This Jesus is "both Lord and [Messiah]" (verse 36).

Judaism Fulfilled

The three thousand newly baptized believers, who soon grew to five thousand and more, were not founding a new religion. They were simply living out the fulfillment of a centuries-old faith in the one true God who had made a promise in the Garden, then to their ancestors, that He would come to deliver them and ultimately the whole world through them.

These new believers were Sabbath-keeping, son-circumcising, Torah-observant, feast-celebrating Jews who now celebrated Jesus as the One who brought meaning to it all. None of these practices ceased when they believed in Yeshua. They still frequented the Temple (see Acts 2:46; 5:12). They were often present at the normal hours of prayer (see 3:1). Even after having been called before the Sanhedrin to defend their faith, they continued daily in the Temple (see 5:42). Ananias, the man who baptized Paul, was a "devout observer of the law" (22:12).

Salvation, however, is not obtained by observing the Law. It is a free gift of God through the vicarious death of the Messiah. Now they could understand why Isaiah had spoken of a "suffering" servant (Isaiah 53:3). Even the feasts and sacrifices took on more meaning. Passover and Pentecost, the Day of Atonement and the Feast of Trumpets were no longer a deliverance of long ago and a holy Law written on stone tablets on Mount Sinai. Rather, they were a recognition of the Messiah who has come, our Passover Lamb, and a law written on our hearts. Just as Jeremiah had predicted—a "new covenant" (31:31–33).

This was not a new religion, this was Judaism fulfilled—filled full! Nor would these believers have answered to the name *Christian*. Not until Antioch (see Acts 11:26) was a believer in Yeshua ever referred to in this hellenized fashion. (The term "Christian" comes from *christos*, the Greek word for Messiah.) No, they were called "Nazarenes"—they followed the Man from Nazareth (see Acts 24:5). They were said to "belong to the Way" (9:2). Others saw them as only another sect of Judaism (see 28:22). Tertullus called Paul a "ringleader of the Nazarene sect" when he was making his accusation before Governor Felix (24:5). But the term "Christian" was reserved for a future day.

Peter's housetop vision at the tanner's house in Joppa and Paul's Damascus Road encounter brought major changes. Gentiles began to be welcomed into the family, and they did not have to become Jews to be accepted.

This was very confusing to a people who had kept themselves scrupulously separate for all those years. A Jerusalem Council had to be called. Some were vehemently opposed to this revelation. "The Gentiles must be circumcised and required to obey the law of Moses," insisted some of the Pharisee believers (Acts 15:5).

There was much discussion and many testimonies before a decision was made. Circumcision and Law-keeping were not necessary for Gentiles. However, they must be very careful to give up pagan customs and unacceptable morals that opposed faith in the one true God (see Acts 15:19–21). The Gentiles were in.

The profile of the body of believers began a rapid transformation. Many Greek names were added to the roster of believers: Gaius, Aristarchus, Trophimus, Theophilos. Cities like Antioch, Ephesus and Rome soon became centers of influence in the ever-expanding family.

Some of Paul's traveling companions were Jewish, some Greek. Timothy, with a Jewish mother and a Greek father, was circumcised before joining Paul's team (see Acts 16:3). On the other hand, there was no such requirement made of Titus, who was fully Greek (see Galatians 2:3).

Jews and Gentiles were learning to live together. A first! But what about Jesus' Jewish followers? Were they now freed from their identity as Abraham's natural seed?

Always a Jew

Paul's special assignment was to Gentiles (see Acts 9:15), yet he never lost his passion for Jews, and he remained an observant Jew for the rest of his life. "I could wish that I myself were cursed and cut off from Christ for the sake of my brothers, those of my own race, the people of Israel," he told the Romans. "My heart's desire and prayer to God . . . is that they may be saved" (9:3–4; 10:1). He was careful to let Gentile churches know that the Gospel was still "first for the Jew" (1:16). When he entered a new city, his first stop was always at the local synagogue—in Salamis, Pisidian Antioch, Iconium, Thessalonica, Berea, Athens, Corinth and Ephesus (see Acts 13:5, 14; 14:1; 17:2, 10, 17; 18:4; 19:8).

Even while a prisoner in Rome, Paul "called together the leaders of the Jews" and "explained and declared to them the kingdom of God and tried to convince them about Jesus from the Law of Moses and from the Prophets" (Acts 28:17, 23). Some were receptive. Some were not. Paul told his nonbelieving brothers that he would now turn to the Gentiles to whom he had been specially sent, and "they will listen" (verse 28).

Jerusalem was always in his heart. Luke tells of a time when, after one of his long journeys, Paul was "in a hurry to reach Jerusalem, if possible, by the day of Pentecost [Shavuot]" (Acts 20:16).

Although Paul meticulously declares that salvation is alone through the finished work of Messiah Yeshua (see Romans 3:21–22), he was a lifelong observer of the now-fulfilled Law and Prophets. "I am a Jew," he told the Roman commander in Jerusalem as he was nearing the end of his life (Acts 21:39). "I am a Pharisee," he reminded the Sanhedrin (23:6). "I believe everything that agrees with the Law and that is written in the Prophets," he told Governor Felix at the Caesarea trial (24:14). "I have done nothing wrong against the law of the Jews or against the temple," he declared to King Festus (25:8). To his Jewish brothers in Rome, he said, "I have done nothing against our people or against the customs of our ancestors" (28:17).

> *Although the apostle Paul meticulously declares that salvation is alone through the finished work of Messiah Yeshua, he was a lifelong observer of the now-fulfilled Law and Prophets.*

Notice that Paul's words were not, "I *was* a Pharisee," but "I *am* a Pharisee." His following Jesus did not negate his heritage nor his credentials.

Yet his loyalty as a Jew was constantly in question. Once, when returning to Jerusalem, Paul was confronted with the rumor that he had turned people away from Moses and was telling Jewish believers not to circumcise their children or to live according to their time-honored traditions. In order to prove that he was still Torah-observant, Paul took a vow. He even paid the expenses of some of the other brothers so that everybody would know that there was no truth in these reports and that he was indeed still living in obedience to the Law (see Acts 21:21–24).

Some have wondered whether Paul did this merely to keep peace among the Jerusalem Jews. If that were the case, it would make Paul out to be a hypocrite, acting one way while in Jerusalem and another way in Ephesus. Clearly this is not the case, yet this man of deep convictions did not try to enforce one culture on another, not even Jewish Torah culture. He insisted to the Galatians that salvation was alone through the finished work of Messiah (see 2:16), though he himself was Torah-observant to the end.

The apostle James in Jerusalem, when urging Paul to take the vow, was quite positive that he [Paul] "stay[ed] in line and [kept] the Torah" (Acts 21:24).[1] "Paul took this vow, not out of compromise, but out of a genuine desire to honor God through keeping Torah,"[2] says Russ Resnik, one of today's resurrected remnant. "Paul still walked in obedience to Torah, but he was not under Torah."[3]

Our Jewish Messiah

Paul made quite a case for the Law, even though he had said, "Christ is the end of the law" (Romans 10:4). The end? How? "The law is holy," he said (7:12). "Is the law sin? Certainly not! Indeed . . . I would not have known what coveting really was if the law had not said, 'Do not covet'" (7:7). "The law is holy, and the commandment is holy, righteous and good" (verse 12). "Do we, then, nullify the law by this faith? Not at all! Rather, we uphold the law" (3:31).

Jesus had made it clear that He did not come to abolish the Law and the Prophets but to fulfill them (see Matthew 5:17). But the Law has never been able to make one righteous. It is only through the Holy Spirit that the "righteous requirements of the law" can be fulfilled (Romans 8:4).

Then what does Paul mean when he says that "Christ is the end of the law"? Perhaps David Stern, a Messianic Jewish scholar, makes it clearer in his translation of this verse. Stern points out that the Greek word *telos,* here translated "end," can equally well be translated "completion, aim, purpose, goal, outcome, or consummation." Writes Stern, "For the goal at which the Torah aims is the Messiah."[4] The Tree of Life version of Scripture is worded in even stronger language: "Messiah is the goal of the Torah as a means to righteousness for everyone who keeps trusting."

Christ is the completion, the goal, the purpose, the aim, the consummation of the Law!

Was this Judaizing? Was Paul's observance of the Law Judaizing? No. Paul was not asking Gentiles to act like Jews even though their only Scripture was the Tanakh, the Hebrew Scriptures. The Judaizers were those who insisted that circumcision and Law observance were the means to righteousness, or those who insisted that Gentiles observe Jewish Law. The finished work of the Messiah is for both Jew and Gentile. Salvation comes by faith in what Messiah has already done—His atoning death on the cross for our sins. Nothing more is needed. Not our sacrifices, not our works. Paul was therefore constantly reminding both Jew and Greek that God "saved us, not because of righteous things we had done, *but because of his mercy*" (Titus 3:5, emphasis mine). Although Jewish believers may still be observers of the Law, it is not the source of their righteousness.

This Jew-Gentile experience seemed to be working. The Jews had known that the Gentiles would one day come to faith in the one true God. It was an essential ingredient in Messiah's mission. Isaiah had foretold it: "The LORD says . . . 'It is too small a thing for you. . . . I will also make you a light for the Gentiles, that you may bring my salvation to the ends of the earth'" (Isaiah 49:5–6).

No, it was no surprise to the Jews. They were simply surprised at the timing. After all, the Jewish Messiah was not yet reigning visibly in Jerusalem. Rome was still in control.

Then something happened that precipitated cataclysmic changes. The tension between Rome and Jerusalem escalated.

Roman armies surrounded the city. The ensuing siege lasted two years, but ultimately the city was destroyed and the Temple lay in ruins.

Jewish believers who remembered the Olivet Discourse (see Matthew 24, Mark 13 and Luke 21) fled across the Jordan to Pella. Their flight accomplished two things: It further separated them from their Jewish brothers who now considered them traitors, perhaps even in league with the Romans, and it further eroded leadership among Jewish believers. Some of the Gentile believers began to interpret the destruction of Jerusalem as God's final judgment on Israel. No doubt, they surmised, He was finished with His "chosen" people, and their promises now belonged to the "Church."

Sixty years later, another historic event sealed the doom of the Jerusalem Jewish Church. The Bar Kokhba revolt of the AD 130s was defeated, and Jews were forbidden to enter the city. As if that were not enough, Emperor Hadrian rebuilt the city, named it Aelia Capitolina and dedicated it to three pagan gods. Any believers left in the city were now Gentiles. They took control of the holy places and entrenched themselves as leaders in the Jerusalem Church.

There were still scattered Jewish believers in the Diaspora—those outside Jerusalem and the Land—until as late as the fourth century, even believers in Messiah in Jewish synagogues, but there was little of Jewish influence left.[5] It is not surprising then that the Gentile Christians understood them less and less.

By the time Shmuel Suran picked up his copy of the Jewish *B'rit Hadashah* in New York City many centuries later, the Jewish connection to the Christian faith was almost forgotten. Few even consider the fact that it is still a Jewish Messiah who even now sits at the right hand of the Father, interceding for us (see Romans 8:34).

The Church has become so Gentile in its practice of faith that those of us who would reclaim a biblical Jewish expression are often considered a little strange—a small price to pay for the re-discovery of our Jewish roots.

Remarks from Marty Goetz,
Messianic singer/songwriter

Reading about Shmuel Suran in Don Finto's book *Your People Shall Be My People* is like reading my own story. Okay—there are some differences. He was born in the "holy land"—New York City—while I was born in Cleveland, Ohio. Apart from that, we share a similar spiritual saga.

Like Shmuel, I, too, was stunned and surprised when I first laid eyes on the opening words of "The Gospel According to Matthew," which I later found out was written specifically for the Jews. For a Jewish person, even to DARE reading past the page in the Bible that states "The New Testament of Our Lord and Savior Jesus Christ" is a bold and risky act. Don's book beautifully lays out some of the reasons for this reality.

I remember making this "leap of faith" way back in 1978. I was en route to Los Angeles, California, from New York City, where I had been living for three years. My pilgrimage to the West Coast was motivated by two things: the first being my desire to become a successful singer/songwriter; the second being my flight from the influence of my ex-singing partner, Bert Lloyd, with whom I had come to New York in pursuit of fame and fortune. On our way to that goal, Bert had gone from being a "good Methodist" to a radically saved, tract-distributing, corner-preaching, Pentecostal, born-again Christian, after attending The Rock Church in Manhattan.

As a young man who grew up in Conservative Judaism, I was horrified by this turn of events. Bert tried to tell me that Jesus was Jewish, that the Scriptures were written by Jews and that the first believers were Jews. He even introduced me to his friend Beth, who claimed to be Jewish. In my mind, she was simply a traitor to our people!

After all, I had been raised by my parents to be a "good Jew," spending countless Sabbath evenings at the home of my Orthodox, Polish-immigrant grandparents, becoming a Bar Mitzvah, chanting from the Torah in Hebrew and singing in the Cantor's Club, the boys' choir that assisted in singing the liturgy at my synagogue. If anyone should know whether Jesus was the Messiah, I should! (Or so I thought!)

So when Bert decided to follow Jesus, I decided to follow my ambition out to Hollywood. On the way to California, I stopped in Cleveland to see my parents. Somehow, I found in their house a big, thick family Bible—you know, the kind that collects dust on coffee tables. It was a strange thing to find in Beachwood, Ohio—a 90 percent Jewish suburb—and to this day, I don't know how it got there! But in my state of mind, I thought it best to take it with me. Perhaps, by reading it, I could find a loophole, an excuse to "unbelieve" the things I had been hearing from Bert and his friends.

In that "dreaded" New Testament, I read the same words Shmuel had read: "The book of the genealogy of Jesus Christ, the Son of David, the Son of Abraham" (Matthew 1:1). And like Shmuel, I thought, *Oy! He's Jewish!*

From then on, I was hooked, making my rounds to music companies in LA by day, only to hurry back to my apartment to read more about this Man who not only was Jewish, but, from what I could see, was a better Jew than I was! I found myself looking up at the sky and asking whoever might be listening that if this Jesus was for the Jews, He—whoever He was—would have to show me. Through a subsequent series of events, He appeared to answer that "prayer."

Sometime later, I found myself reluctantly yet irresistibly drawn down the aisle of a church to give my heart to Yeshua! I was led in a prayer of confession, received a smaller

Bible and was welcomed into the family of God. With much joy—and horror—I had become a "born-again Christian."

What I REALLY had become was something I later put into song: "A Jew Born Anew." Like Shmuel, I was simply a Jewish man who, through the prayers and faithful witness of Christians who cared about me, had met my Messiah—the Messiah OF and FOR Israel!

The "Gentilizing"
of the Church

God has granted even the Gentiles repentance unto life.

Acts 11:18

Recently, while in Spain with a friendship group of Jews and Gentiles, I visited historical sites of anti-Jewish legislation and persecution in former years. In Granada we stood in the Ambassador Room of the Alhambra Palace, where Ferdinand and Isabella had signed the 1492 decree to evict Jews and confiscate their property. Here we were revisiting events, confessing sins and asking for forgiveness on behalf of ancestors long dead, whose decisions have continued to affect us to this day.

These were very emotional gatherings, but nothing had prepared us for what we would see when, in Toledo, we rounded the corner of an ancient street and came upon San Juan de los Reyes. Hanging from the walls of this old monastery were the chains with which Jewish people had been tortured and killed five centuries earlier—stark reminders of a dark past. This was not an abandoned building. Grains of rice were strewn on the cobblestones outside the cathedral, where a bridal party had been celebrating earlier that day.

Why were the chains still hanging there? Why had they not been removed? Our small band was struck dumb. Embarrassed, ashamed and stunned, we bowed our heads and backed away. And yet in the throes of grief and shame, I remember a kind of numbness in my heart as if there was no way to emote deeply enough to express what ought to be felt at such a time.

Around the corner was a small park. We shuffled toward the area and huddled together, still in speechless consternation. Then one of our Jewish mothers sat down on the ground and began to throw dust on her head, her way of expressing the inexpressible. I sat beside her, following her lead. Others, Jew and Gentile, held each other. After a long season of silence, someone began saying *Kaddish*—the Jewish prayer for the dead—honoring the Jewish men, women and children who had been tormented and murdered by past generations of "Christians."

Back in the first century, the Jewish believers had graciously received us Gentiles as equals in the family. But we had rejected them. How had it come to this?

Paul, the apostle to the Gentiles, had begun to see danger signs in the last days of his life. "Do not boast over those branches," he had warned the Romans. "If you do, consider this: You do not support the root, but the root supports you. Do not be arrogant" (Romans 11:18, 20).

But arrogant we have been! Paul's admonition has gone unheeded for almost twenty centuries.

Who Killed the Messiah?

By the time of Origen, about the middle of the third century, it was an accepted belief among most Christians that the destruction of Jerusalem and the dispersion of the Jews were God's method of showing the world that He was finished with them. They "will never be restored to their former condition. For they have committed a crime of the most unhallowed kind, in conspiring against the Saviour of the human race," Origen wrote in *Against Celsus*.[1]

What had happened to Romans 11:1 and 11? "Did God reject his people? By no means! Did they stumble so as to fall beyond recovery? Not at all!" And what about Jeremiah? Had Origen and others overlooked his prophecy that Israel would be a nation as long as the sun is in the sky (see Jeremiah 31:35–37)?

Did Jews *alone* "conspire against the Savior"? Was it not Pilate, a Gentile, who had to give the last word? And what about the Roman soldiers? Following orders? Yes. But actively involved in His arrest, torture and crucifixion.

Nonetheless, the Church was not taking any chances. Emperor Constantine called the Nicene Council in AD 325 to solve some of the doctrinal problems, but he also wanted to make sure that the Church had once and for all separated herself from these "polluted wretches" who had stained their hands with a "nefarious crime."[2] They needed a resurrection celebration date other than Passover. Passover was too Jewish!

"It appeared an unworthy thing that in the celebration of this most holy feast, we should follow the practice of the Jews, who have impiously defiled their hands with an enormous sin, and are, therefore, deservedly afflicted with blindness of soul," wrote Constantine to the assembled bishops in Nicea.[3]

At the conclusion of the Council meeting, Constantine had his way and celebrated with a huge church banquet. The Roman calendar had conquered. The annual celebration of the Lord's resurrection would now have a new name—Easter—strangely similar to *Eostre*, the Teutonic goddess of spring, dissimilar to *Pesach* or Passover, the festival of its origin. God's calendar for the Passover was subjugated by the Western Church from that point forward.

The prophet Daniel had envisioned four great beasts and a king that would "change the set times and the laws" (7:25). In his insistence that the Church change the calendar of God, Constantine became a foreshadowing of another world ruler who is to come. And the Church was further estranged from her roots and her spiritual "parents."

"It is into their place that ye have been set," John Chrysostom assured his flock a few years later.[4] Jewish people who had come to faith were now expected to renounce everything Jewish. If they refused, they were considered heretics and came under the ire of a confused Gentile Church.

Further generations of theologians accepted the "replacement theory" as doctrine.[5] Jeremiah and Paul were forgotten; their clear words reinterpreted.

By the time of the Second Nicene Council in AD 787, believing Jews had to prove they were "Christians." They were, for example, refused Communion by decree of the Church Council unless they forsook the observance of the Sabbath or any other Jewish custom. In some cases they had to prove their disdain for their roots by eating pork in front of witnesses.[6]

The Lateran Councils of AD 1179 and AD 1215 ordered Jews to live in separate quarters and to wear distinctive dress. This paved the way for ghetto living and the yellow badge required prior to and during the time of the Nazi Holocaust.

Martin Luther brought hope to millions through the Reformation movement of the sixteenth century. Paul's letter to the Romans had brought him life. But Luther seems to have gleaned nothing from Romans 11:28–29: "As far as the gospel is concerned, they [the Jews] are enemies on your account; but as far as election is concerned, they are loved on account of the patriarchs, for God's gifts and his call are irrevocable." Luther's comments? "The word 'enemies' must here be taken in a passive sense, that is, they [the Jews] deserve to be hated. God hates them, and so they are hated by the Apostles and all who are of God."[7]

God hates them? Just the opposite. Rather, Paul says, "They are loved." Earlier in the same chapter, Paul says that they are not rejected. They have not fallen beyond recovery. They will rise again. It will be a time of great riches.

As much as Luther did to bring about a reformed Church, he helped advance further disdain for this chosen family of God. Years later, Hitler did not have to look far to find justification for his hatred of the Jews. Luther is quoted in the evil dictator's classic work *Mein Kampf*!

During these years there was no place of safety for a Jewish believer. Either he kept quiet about his faith and remained in his local synagogue—thus denying his Lord—or he acknowledged his faith and was forced out of the Jewish fellowship into the strange world of the Gentiles, losing all future identity as a Jew.

I wonder, too, about the people who once hung from those chains on the side of San Juan de los Reyes. Were they Jews who had been forced to pledge allegiance to an invisible king they did not even know? Or were they Jewish believers who had refused to give up being Jewish? I can close my eyes and still see them. Silent, gruesome witnesses of a fallen Church.

As for who killed the Messiah? The sins of Adam's entire family were on Messiah's shoulders that day on the cross. Our sins nailed Him there. He came to redeem both Jew and Gentile, and it was both Jew and Gentile who condemned Him to death.

The Estrangement Continues

In our own century, the idea that the Church has replaced Israel has so permeated our thinking that even recently published Bibles often contain marginal notes and chapter headings that continue to support this ancient error that results in hatred of the Jews.

One well-known Bible dictionary, in commenting on Paul and his relationship to his Jewishness, states:

Paul argued that the Jews had forfeited these promises, which had come to Abraham through faith, not the law (Rom. 4:13). Because "it is men of faith who are the [true] sons of Abraham" (Gal. 3:7), Christians, not Jews, could now claim to be descended from the Israelite patriarchs. The Church was, in fact "the twelve tribes in the Dispersion" (Jas. 1:1)."[8]

> *The idea that the Church has replaced Israel has so permeated our thinking that even recently published Bibles often support this ancient error that results in hatred of the Jews.*

In this excellent dictionary, the words of Paul have been used to declare what Paul had clearly denied—that the Gentiles have replaced Israel. Paul was indeed insisting it is faith, not self-righteous adherence to the Law, that saves. But in no place does he or James call Gentiles "the twelve tribes in the Dispersion."

One study Bible,[9] in all other points a fine work, points out the widespread acceptance of the spiritual demise of Israel and the ascendancy of the Church. For example, the chapter headings for Isaiah read:

Isaiah 41—*God speaks of his merciful providence in regard to his church*

Isaiah 43—*The Lord comforts the church with his promises*

Isaiah 52—*The church roused with God's promise of free redemption*

Isaiah 60—*Glory of the church in the abundant access of the Gentiles*

Isaiah 65—*The Gentiles called. The Jews rejected. A remnant saved. Blessed state of the new Jerusalem.*

The headings at the top of the pages make this emphasis even more obvious:

God's mercies to the church
God's promises to the church
The restoration of the church
The prophet's zeal for the church
Confession and complaint of the church

With these constant references to the Church, even though the Church is never mentioned in any of these chapters, the real subject of Israel is overlooked.

Listen to this statement from another of today's writers: "'The nation that will not serve us will perish' (Isaiah 60:12); 'all the peoples of the earth will be subdued under our feet' (Psalm 47:1–3)—promises made originally to Israel, but now to be fulfilled in the New Israel, the Church."[10]

The promises made to Israel are indeed available to Gentiles, but only as they come into covenant with and partner with redeemed Israel. Paul makes it very plain that those who were Gentiles by birth and separated from Christ, "excluded from citizenship in Israel and foreigners to the covenants of the promise" had been included through the blood of Messiah. "Consequently, you are no longer foreigners and aliens, but fellow citizens with God's people and members of God's household" (Ephesians 2:12, 19).

We Gentiles have become citizens of Israel. That is our only access to Israel's promises. Once we were "foreigners to the covenants of the promise," but that day is past. Israel's Messiah is now our Messiah.[11]

We have made it difficult for the Jewish people to receive Him. We make demands that hold them back. The history of confusion is very long, the wounds very deep.

One group of modern theologians thinks we should no longer desire to tell the Jews about Jesus. These scholars have developed a whole new theology—a so-called Dual Covenant—the idea that the Jews do not need Jesus, they are saved through their covenant with Abraham and only the Gentiles are saved through Jesus.

What a travesty!

It is not enough that we have turned our backs on these closest of kin to Jesus. Now we have decided they do not need their own Messiah!

That is no answer. Jesus is Messiah of both Jew and Gentile or He is not Messiah at all.

Any true Christian deplores contrived conversions and manipulative witnessing techniques. We abhor intimidation. We grieve over our past. But yes, the Jewish people still need a Savior, as do we. We love the Jews. We bless them. We protect them in persecution. We make no demands of them. But He is their Messiah, too. We dare not forget that fact.

"Jerusalem will be trampled on by the Gentiles until the times of the Gentiles are fulfilled" (Luke 21:24)! Prophetic words indeed. Yet none of Jesus' hearers could have imagined what would transpire over the next years: that the Gentiles would take control of the books of Moses and the Prophets—so much so that the Bible, God's inspired Word, would be appropriated by Gentiles for themselves to the extent that it is now known primarily as a Gentile book; that this Man in whom they now believed, this Messiah, this Christ, would become so "Gentilized" that even His own people would fail to recognize Him as one of their own; that millions of Jews in the twentieth century would be killed at the hands of those who gave lip service to their Messiah.

Yeshua, Son of David, Son of God, had now become Jesus Christ, Savior of the Gentiles. In earlier times, the Jews had received us into their family, but we now rejected them. In the heart of the Church, the Gentiles were in but the Jews were out.

The Church assumed that all was well, but the Lord was not pleased with the rejection. There was a price to be paid. The people who had rejected God's choice family would not even find unity among themselves.

Remarks from Eitan Shishkoff,
Tents of Mercy, Kiryat Yam, Israel

We'd have been burned at the stake if my wife and I had lived during the era in Spain described by Don in this chapter! Instead, other Messianic Jews (followers of Jesus who live openly as Jews) and I are invited to churches and conferences of Christians around the world to explain and celebrate the Jewish roots of New Testament faith. Now, after some nineteen centuries of anti-Semitic ex cathedra rulings, many Church leaders are opening their arms to us, honoring the Jewish people and standing with the resurgent Messianic Jewish movement.

The Church fathers—Martin Luther and countless other theologians—would find it strange to walk into many Christian sanctuaries today. They would hear Hebrew songs praising God, watch Jewish folk dance, see banners displaying the star of David and listen to the sound of the *shofar* (the ram's horn blown during Old Testament times). What has changed? It is simply and profoundly, as Don Finto points out, the fulfillment of Romans 11:12, 15: "Now if their fall is riches for the world, and their failure riches for the Gentiles, how much more their fullness. . . . For if their being cast away is the reconciling of the world, what will their acceptance be but life from the dead?" With supernatural foresight, Paul prophesies an era when the "natural (Jewish) branches" of God's olive tree will be grafted back in, bringing fresh life and wholeness to the entire household of faith.

In Israel, where I live, Arab and Jewish believers in Messiah gather to worship together, respecting and affirming each other's cultural expression. It is indeed a new day. Yet, as Don documented in this chapter, much of the Church is still caught in the deception that the Church replaces Israel.

If only they knew the joy of the Father in welcoming His Jewish sons and daughters back to His house!

Christians have a choice. I believe it's the same choice put before the "stay-at-home" son in Luke 15. When the prodigal returned after a long absence, his father rejoiced and threw a party. Resentment gripped the brother who remained at home. "He should come back quietly, without fanfare. After all, he has brought disrepute to our father [read Ezekiel 36:22–30 regarding our exile from the Land, bringing shame to the God of Israel]." But "Dad" would have none of it and chided the critical brother, who by now felt that he had replaced the prodigal! His father's corrective exhortation? "Let's celebrate. Your brother was dead and is alive; was lost and now is found." I can't imagine a clearer picture of the dead bones Ezekiel saw coming to life (37:1–14) or the light of God shining upon rebirthed Israel and drawing the Gentile nations (Isaiah 60:1–3).

The reappearance of Jesus' Jewish disciples in our time is nothing less than a resurrection that portends His dramatic return. This book is a tool to bring balanced, biblical understanding to a miracle happening before our eyes. As I wrote in *What About Us?*, the key to spiritual health and power for the reunited Jewish and Gentile believers in the twenty-first century is mutual blessing and security. I don't need to become a Gentile (the error of the "replacement" teaching and dominant practice of the Church from the second to the twentieth centuries). And my Christian brother/sister does not need to become a Jew (as made clear in the Acts 15 ruling). Together, we can rejoice in the rich, ancient roots of our shared faith in Yeshua.

How thrilling to be living in a day that the prophets and apostles eagerly anticipated! May we take our place in the drama in a way that pleases the Father's heart.

Division—The DNA of the Gentile Church

A man reaps what he sows.

Galatians 6:7

The early believers "were together and had everything in common" (Acts 2:44). They were "one in heart and mind" (4:32). In the Garden of Gethsemane, Jesus prayed that all of us may be one so "that the world may believe that you have sent me" (John 17:21).

But we are *not* one. There are now hundreds of different ecclesiastical traditions with multiple thousands of separate and distinct denominations within the larger Body of Christ!

The natural law inherent in all of God's creation—the DNA, so to speak—has had its effect on the Church. We have reproduced "according to our kind" (see Genesis 1:11). By breaking from those who birthed us, the Church has produced one division after another. Every new movement has resulted in a new church; each reformation, a new denomination. Nineteen centuries later we have: Eastern Orthodox and Roman Catholic; Anglican and Protestant; Calvinism and Arminianism; Lutheran, Baptist, Methodist, Nazarene and Pentecostal; denominationalism and nondenominationalism.

There is still a family resemblance, but a mutation has entered our bloodstream. Mutations may produce only a slight change in the first generation but can ultimately bring about "great changes such as severe deformities or diseases."[1]

By breaking from those who birthed us, the Church has produced one division after another. Every new movement has resulted in a new church; each reformation, a new denomination.

It all began with that first break when the Gentile Church assumed a superior position. According to Marty Waldman:

The gaping wound of the schism between Jews and Gentiles represents the "grand-daddy" of all wounds in the Body of Messiah. All other wounds of division in the Church stem from this original wound. Because the Church had grown to believe that it superseded Israel and Messianic Judaism, the spirit of supersessionism has plagued Christianity through the ages. The Orthodox Church believes that the Roman Catholic Church is in rebellion. The Roman Catholic Church has always viewed the Protestants as religious rebels. The many denominations and divisions in the Protestant Church are primarily the result of one group of Christians superseding an existing group because they have found a "more pure way." Supersessionism essentially nullifies the promise of God to the previous group.[2]

It was Moses who first heard God say, "Israel is my firstborn son" (Exodus 4:22). A firstborn son has an irreplaceable position of honor in the family. Paul was specifically speaking of Israel when he said, "God's gifts and his call are irrevocable" (Romans 11:29).

Gentile Christians—the Stay-at-Home Son

In the gospel of Luke, Jesus tells the story of the Prodigal Son, in which the younger son leaves home, goes into a foreign country and squanders his inheritance (see Luke 15:11–31). Much later he "came to his senses" (verse 17) and started home. "But while he was still a long way off, his father saw him and was filled with compassion for him; he ran to his son, threw his arms around him and kissed him" (verse 20). There was a royal celebration. "This son of mine was dead and is alive again," the father rejoiced (verse 24).

But the older son was irate. His brother had lost his inheritance and that should be the end of it. There was certainly no cause for feasting. This younger rebel brother had gotten what he deserved in the pigsty of the "far country." Now everything should belong to *him,* the faithful older son. "*I've* been the one who has slaved for you all these years and never disobeyed your orders," he reminded their father, "and you've never thrown a big party for *me!*" (verse 29, author's paraphrase).

The Gentile saga is this story in reverse. The firstborn son, Israel, left home. The younger brother, the Gentiles, stayed with the Father. As far as they were concerned, the firstborn was disowned and is now to be regarded as an enemy. The son who remained at home assumed he had supplanted the missing brother in all matters, including the place of intimate fellowship with the Father.

After centuries of wandering, Israel is finally on the way home, but the Church is not happy. "They had their chance," we seem to be saying. "They squandered their inheritance. Now it's our time. They no longer have any rights in Father's house."

On the other hand, Father is saying, "Quick! Bring the best robe and put it on him. Put a ring on his finger and sandals on his feet. Bring the fattened calf and kill it. Let's have a feast and celebrate" (verses 22–23).

Eitan Shishkoff and I once shared an unforgettable moment that has further bonded us in our mutual covenant of faith. Having been asked to speak to a Messianic Jewish conference, we were both seated on the platform.

Eitan rose, made his remarks and sat down. While I was addressing this predominantly Jewish crowd, encouraging both Jewish believers to keep the vision and Gentiles to stand alongside their new brothers and sisters in Yeshua, the familiar parable of the Prodigal Son—with a surprising twist—surfaced in my consciousness. Suddenly I saw myself as the "stay-at-home" Gentile, the son of the Church, who has maligned, ridiculed, persecuted and rejected her brother, Israel. With crushing intensity, I felt the massive burden of guilt for generations of my ancestors.

In this moment of awakening, I also saw Eitan as the son of the persecuted race. It was so clear to me that he must always be bearing the grief of millions of relatives annihilated through the centuries. Reaching back, I drew him forward, then fell on my knees at his feet, shaking and sobbing. "Forgive us! Forgive us!" I cried, the sins of those centuries on my shoulders.

We Gentiles are the spiritual descendants of the Jewish people. "Salvation is from the Jews," Jesus told the Samaritan woman at the well (John 4:22). He—the Jew—is our "parent" in the faith. Without Jewish faith, there would be no Christianity.

It occurred to me one day as I was rereading the Ten Commandments in light of this issue that there may be more than meets the eye in the fifth commandment (Deuteronomy 5:16): "Honor your father and your mother," the Lord commanded—"which is the first commandment with a promise," Paul adds in his letter to the Ephesians (6:2). Why? "That it may go well with you and that you may enjoy long life on the earth" (verse 3).

Could it be, I wondered, that long, fulfilling spiritual life is being withheld from the Church until she honors the origins of her faith? Could it be that our history of division will cease only after we unite with God's chosen family? Marty Waldman thinks so. He believes that the reemergence in our day of the Messianic Jewish community is the provision of God to address this great wound of division so that true healing can be brought to the Church.

Our Bloodstained Hands

God often requires confession of sin and restitution to be made for the sins of former generations.

Soon after David became king over all Israel, there was a three-year famine. Perplexed over this crisis, "David sought the face of the LORD. The LORD said, 'It is on account of Saul and his blood-stained house; it is because he put the Gibeonites to death'" (2 Samuel 21:1).

Saul? What did Saul, who was now dead, have to do with David? David was not responsible for Saul's sins, was he? And the Gibeonites? That was a reference to a covenant made by Joshua hundreds of years earlier (see Joshua 9). Could that long-ago broken promise be affecting David's reign? Could yesterday's sins really be the cause of today's famine?

Yes! That is exactly what God was telling David.

As Israel entered the land, their leader, Joshua, made a covenant with the Gibeonites. Four hundred years later, Saul, the first king of Israel, broke that covenant. The famine that blighted the land during David's reign came because Saul had dishonored and killed a covenant people. This godless deed, committed centuries later, now rested on the head of the present ruler, and God expected an appropriate act of contrition and confession.

The Church finds herself in a similar place today. Past generations of leaders have dishonored and even killed this special people whom God marked for blessing. We are the descendants, both physically and spiritually, of those generations. Authority has now passed to us just as it did to David. From us, as well, the

Lord expects humility, acknowledgment of sin and appropriate action before the curse can be removed.

If the spiritual famine of our day is to be stopped, if the "greater riches" revival is to escalate, if this "life from the dead" for God's chosen is to continue, then we must extend hands of petition to a forgiving God, hands of healing to a wounded people.

"Thy kingdom come! Thy will be done on earth as it is in heaven," we have been praying for these hundreds of years. The Church has known its moments of glory as we have traversed the continents to tell the world of its Redeemer. But we have never come into our fullness. Too often, our prayers have risen from hate-filled hearts and bloodstained hands.

Welcome Home!

The Church is coming to grips with her sins. Reconciliation groups are meeting in every nation. Germans are confessing to Europeans, Japanese to Asians, descendants of European conquerors to indigenous people groups, sons and daughters of former slaveholders and slave traders to sons and daughters of former slaves.

The Jewish issues are no longer being ignored. I am a part of a group that calls itself the Toward Jerusalem Council II. We use the word *Toward* because we know we are looking forward to a time when an official church council will be called. We use the words *Jerusalem Council II* because this will be a follow-up of the original council described in Acts 15. In that assembly the Jewish believers met to decide how to welcome Gentiles without requiring that they become Jews. The Toward Jerusalem Council II will be a Gentile council called to decide how to welcome back Jews without requiring that they act like Gentiles. Our group wants "to repair and heal the breach between Jewish and Gentile believers in Yeshua, dating from the first centuries of the

Church, and to do so primarily through humility, prayer, and repentance."³

We have traveled to Spain, to Rome, to Nicea (Turkey), to Israel. We have visited with key leaders of historic churches as well as leaders of evangelical and charismatic churches. We have stood together in the ruins of Nicea, where Gentiles formed a receiving line to welcome our Jewish brothers. It was our attempt to make amends for the fact that they had not been invited to the AD 325 and the AD 787 councils!

In Spain, in an act of repentance for the decree made in Elvira in AD 306—that Christians were not to receive blessings from Jews—Spanish Christians asked our Jewish brothers to bless them and their fields.

For four hours we prayed at the ruins of Yavneh, where Jewish leaders met in the late first century to decide how the faith should continue without the Jerusalem Temple.

From the Mount of Olives we looked out over the city of Jerusalem and prayed again Jesus' prayer for the city. Then we lifted our eyes heavenward to tell Him that we, too, were anticipating the time when a great host of His own nearest of kin would welcome Him back.

As the Church is beginning to welcome the Jewish people back to their ancestral home, a spiritual awakening is also stirring among this Jacob family. Simultaneously, the unity among believers in the Church, across every denominational barrier, is growing. The most rapidly advancing churches are those that are no longer bound by denominational fervor but by devotion to the King. It is happening as the Lord prayed. As brothers and sisters in this huge spiritual family come together, millions more will come to faith. But the family can only come together as we remember our elder brother, the one through whom our Redeemer has been revealed.

All of this will continue as Israel returns to her ancestral home, just as the prophets foretold.

Remarks from Asher Intrater,
Revive Israel, Jerusalem, Israel

To understand the importance of God's covenants with Israel, one should first understand that the emphasis is not on our specialness but on His faithfulness. Through God's covenants with Israel, He demonstrates His character. God shows His greatness through being gracious to sinners, generous to the poor, powerful to the enemies, faithful to the unfaithful.

His faithfulness to the Jewish people over thousands of years shows His attitude toward covenant, His commitment to long-term relationships. As He is faithful to the first covenant people, so will He be faithful to others. Were He not faithful to them, He would not be faithful to others. The demonstration of God's extraordinary faithfulness to the Jewish people should be a benchmark of confidence and assurance to every person desiring to trust God in any nation, in any generation.

"Will their lack of faith cancel the faithfulness of God? Certainly not!" (Romans 3:3–4).

As we see God's faithfulness to the Jewish people, we are encouraged to be faithful to our relationships as well. As He is committed to covenant, so are we to be faithful. We are committed to faithfulness in marriage, to unity in our congregations, to loyalty in our friendships. As we develop the godly character of faithfulness in our own lives, the more it will be obvious that God is faithful, including His covenants with the Jewish people. If we do not act in faithfulness ourselves, we may have a hard time expecting God to be faithful to others.

It would seem that if we do not see God's faithfulness to the people of Israel, there would be little basis for our being faithful to one another. When the international Church lost its covenant loyalty to the people of Israel, it lost its own sense of loyalty among its own streams and divisions.

The first division of the Kingdom of God may be seen as the split between Judah and Israel, and the second great division as the split between Israel and the Church. There is a great prophecy in Ezekiel that God will one day unite the split between Judah and Israel as the prophet joined two trees or pieces of wood together in his hands: "I will take the wood of Joseph which is in the hand of Ephraim and the tribes of Israel, his friends, and I will put them on him, the wood of Judah; and I will make them one tree; and they will become one in My hand" (37:19). [The word in Hebrew (*ets*, עֵץ) may at times refer to a stick, tree, wood, scaffold and even a cross.]

As God promises to join in unity the split between Judah and Israel, we may believe on a similar basis that He will join Jew and Gentile together in one, and unite the various divisions in the international Church as well. God's commitment to His covenants with Israel is the basis for our faith in unity and reconciliation among the nations as well. As Ezekiel united the two pieces of wood, so are all of us united through the wood of the cross of Yeshua the Messiah.

8

Return to the Land

Who are these that fly along like clouds, like doves to their nests?

Isaiah 60:8

I will take the Israelites out of the nations where they have
gone. I will gather them from all around and bring them back
into their own land. I will make them one nation in the land.

Ezekiel 37:21–22

It must have been a strange sight. We did not look like gardeners.
Yet there we were, about twenty of us, standing on a rather barren
hillside outside the city of Jerusalem, spades in one hand, tiny tree
seedlings in the other. We set about digging holes in the ground,
where we placed the plants, then packed the earth tightly around
them before giving them a drink. Each tree honored someone we
loved. For every tree planted, we paid ten dollars to the government of Israel.

Suddenly the whole scene struck some of us as hilarious. After paying the price of the tour, we were now paying additional money for the privilege of planting trees—trees that neither we nor the people being honored were likely ever to see again. What a chamber of commerce this Israeli government has! What other nation has ever conceived of such a revenue-producing plan?

But this nation is different; no other can compare. The title deed to their property was signed by the Almighty Himself. Israel was to be considered the "center of the nations" (Ezekiel 5:5). In fact, "when the Most High divided to the nations their inheritance, when he separated the sons of Adam, he set the bounds of the people according to the number of the children of Israel" (Deuteronomy 32:8 KJV). We may be working on that one for a while, but that's what the Book says!

The psalmist calls Israel "the people close to his [God's] heart" (Psalm 148:14). "To your descendants I give this land," God promised Abraham (Genesis 15:18), then "signed" a covenant of blood (see Genesis 15:1–20). "To you and your descendants I will give all these lands and will confirm the oath I swore to your father Abraham," the Lord later restated to Isaac (26:3). And to Jacob, after changing his name to Israel, He said, "The land I gave to Abraham and Isaac I also give to you, and I will give this land to your descendants after you" (35:12).

"This land"? Which land? The Lord was amazingly precise in defining its borders and boundaries: "From the river of Egypt to the great river, the Euphrates" was His word to Abraham (Genesis 15:18). To the conquering Joshua, four hundred years later, He further clarified: "Your territory will extend from the desert to Lebanon, and from the great river, the Euphrates—all the Hittite country—to the Great Sea on the west" (Joshua 1:4).

The extent of God's land promise is shocking for today's readers. How can it ever be possible that Israel will extend all the way to the Euphrates? Can it be that all or parts of Syria, Egypt, Lebanon, Jordan, Iraq and Iran will one day belong to Israel? What horrific upheaval must take place before that can happen? I do not know the answer, but I ask you to remember that one of the theses of this book is that we take the Word literally unless there is reason to interpret it figuratively. And to assume that the land of Israel will be less than the prophetically defined dimensions of Joshua 1:4 is unwise, particularly in light of the expanding borders of the Land just in the past fifty years.[1]

For how long was this land covenant, this deed, to be valid? That stipulation is exact. "For a thousand generations [that's at least forty thousand years], the covenant he made with Abraham, the oath he swore to Isaac. He confirmed it to Jacob . . . an everlasting covenant" (1 Chronicles 16:15–17). But what covenant? "I will give the land of Canaan as the portion you will inherit" (verse 18).

This phenomenal covenant of land and love carried with it certain conditions. "If you do not carefully follow all the words of this law . . . you will be uprooted from the land. . . . Then the LORD will scatter you among all nations, from one end of the earth to the other" (Deuteronomy 28:58–64). Luke called it being "taken as prisoners to all the nations" (21:24). This would be the penalty for Israel's unfaithfulness.

Jewish history, for almost twenty centuries, has proven these words true. It all started when the Assyrians conquered the northern kingdom in 721 BC. The influential leaders were exiled and dispersed, never to return. Jerusalem and the southern kingdom endured for almost 150 years before the Babylonian invasion destroyed both the city and the Temple. After a 70-year exile, some Israelites returned and the Temple was rebuilt. Then the Romans took over rule and destroyed the Temple in AD 70. And for nearly two thousand years, there was no nation of Israel.

The desolation of the Land, described by Isaiah, was complete. "The cities lie ruined and without inhabitant . . . the houses are left deserted and the fields ruined and ravaged" (6:11). The nation of Israel was, as Ezekiel had prophesied, a valley of dry bones (see 37:1–2).

In the Spirit, the prophet Ezekiel saw that valley full of bones come to life. As he was prophesying, the bones came together. A second prophecy called forth the breath. As Ezekiel prophesied, the whole valley came to life and stood to their feet—"a vast army" (37:10).

As mentioned in a previous chapter, Ezekiel's vision has been used repeatedly to describe a dead Church that needs revival. But the prophet was not seeing a Church; he was seeing Israel. Were we to question that interpretation, the Lord does not leave us in doubt. "These bones are the whole house of Israel," the Lord assured Ezekiel. "I will settle [them] in [their] own land" (verses 11, 14).

This risen-from-the-dead nation was no longer to be two nations as it was prior to the Assyrian and Babylonian conquests. "They will never again be two nations or be divided into two kingdoms" (verse 22). Both Jeremiah and Hosea had been given similar revelations. "The house of Judah will join the house of Israel" (Jeremiah 3:18). "The people of Judah and the people of Israel will be reunited, and they will appoint one leader" (Hosea 1:11). Thus unified, they will live and work together in harmony.

Return of the Remnant

The return of the dispersed people of Israel is to be "from the four quarters of the earth" (Isaiah 11:12), not just from the East—from Babylon—as was the return in 516 BC. Isaiah makes it clear that this is to be a second return and that it will include immigrants from the north, south, east and west. Isaiah even named some of the lands—Egypt, Africa (Cush) and Babylon—but other regions, referred to as "the islands of the sea" (verse 11), were unknown to him at the time of his writing.

Ships would come "bringing [their] sons from afar" (Isaiah 60:9). Others would "fly along like clouds, like doves to their nests" (verse 8), a prophetic reference to air traffic that would fill the skies

2,600 years after Isaiah's time! It was to be a greater exodus than
the earlier one from Egypt (see Jeremiah 23:7–8). The north was
specifically pointed out as a land from which many immigrants
would come. How interesting that today, one out of seven Israelis
is Russian. (Moscow is virtually due north of Jerusalem.)

"Expectant mothers and women in labor" (Jeremiah 31:8) would
be among those returning. When the Yemen Jews arrived in 1950,
twelve babies had been born in flight, five in the Ethiopian airlift
of May 1991.

The wilderness has burst into bloom (see Isaiah 35:1–2). Desert
fortunes are being restored. Vineyards have been planted on the
hills of Samaria (see Jeremiah 31:5)—what the news media calls
the West Bank.

Wealth from other nations is being invested in Israel (see Isaiah
60:5). Even our little tree-planting venture that day brought in
some of that wealth.

The return would not be without a struggle. "I will say to the
north, 'Give them up!' and to the south, 'Do not hold them back.'
Bring my sons from afar and my daughters from the ends of the
earth" (Isaiah 43:6). "I will send for many fishermen . . . and they
will catch them. After that I will send for many hunters, and they
will hunt them down" (Jeremiah 16:16).

Even leaving the Diaspora and returning to the Land is to be a
time when "cries of fear are heard—terror, not peace" (Jeremiah
30:5). All these details of amazing accuracy were written by the
prophets so many years ago and are fulfilled or are being fulfilled
in our day!

The Story of Eliezer Urbach

One son of Israel who encountered great difficulty in returning
to Israel is Eliezer Urbach.[2] I met Eliezer while attending a Jewish
meeting in New Mexico. I had heard about this man who, with his

younger brother Ernest, fled from his home in Skoczow, Poland, in September of 1939, when German warplanes and soldiers stormed that country. To escape capture, Eliezer and Ernest swam across an icy river, hid in forests and avoided Nazi search dogs on their way to the Russian sector. They arrived there, thinking themselves safe under Communism, only to find that Jewish people were also unwanted in Russia. The two brothers were sent off to a Siberian labor camp, where Ernest later died.

After years of starvation and deprivation, Eliezer was ultimately released from the Siberian prison so that the state would not have to bury his malnourished body. But his flight to freedom was far from over.

He found his way first to Uzbekistan and then was jailed again in Afghanistan before reaching his hometown. To his horror he discovered that, in his absence, his entire family had been sent to the gas ovens of Auschwitz, just thirty miles from his village.

Hoping to find a way to survive his personal holocaust, Eliezer joined the Russian army but was arrested for smuggling Jewish people to safety. On his way to a court martial, he escaped to Munich, Germany, and sought refuge with an uncle who lived in that city. There he found neither a safe haven nor a gracious welcome.

Pushing on to Paris in his quest for freedom, Eliezer connected with one of the Jewish committees formed to aid immigrants.[3] With their help and at one point disguised as a British soldier, he ultimately arrived in "Palestine" just in time to fight in the War of Independence of 1948.

As I looked into Eliezer's bearded, weathered face, deeply carved with pain and suffering, I saw the collective grief of multiple thousands who have died at sea, been held captive in detention camps, scaled mountains, swum rivers and endured every imaginable hardship to reach this land of insecure borders and tenuous freedom.

But I saw something else. Peace was etched across his countenance. Love and compassion shone from his eyes. How was this possible? Forced by the hardships of modern Israel's first years—the early '50s—Eliezer went to Brazil. Invited by a kind Gentile to read the New Covenant, he did. There, after many brushes with death, he found life. He found both the God and the Messiah of Israel.

The First Aliyah

The first *aliyah*—return to the Land—occurred in the late nineteenth century. In 1882, according to the Jewish census records, there were only about 24,000 Jewish residents of "Palestine" living in seventeen agricultural colonies. One of the early pioneers was another Eliezer—Eliezer ben-Yehuda—who spent every waking hour pulling together what would become the resurrected Hebrew language. Another early settler was Polish-born David Green, who later took the name David ben Gurion and became Israel's first prime minister.

But the man who is given credit for the rebirth of the nation was a young secular Jewish Viennese newspaperman named Theodor Herzl. In Paris, in January 1895, he was present at the public humiliation of Captain Alfred Dreyfus, the only Jew on the general staff of the French army, falsely accused of espionage. As Dreyfus was sentenced, the chants of the crowd changed from "Kill the traitor!" to "Kill the Jew!"[4]

Herzl left that city with an urgency to establish a safe place for Jewish people. Two years later he convened the First World Zionist Congress in Basel, Switzerland. At that first meeting a national flag was selected for Israel—the blue and white of the prayer shawl—and a national anthem was chosen, *"Hatikvah,"* meaning "The Hope." An elected Jewish executive was chosen to guide the movement, and a Jewish national bank and a land bank were created with which to begin buying land in the area of the new state.

Perhaps the next really significant piece of the fulfillment of Theodor Herzl's dream came through the work of a Jewish scientist named Chaim Weizman, who had produced a synthetic acetone used in gunpowder needed by the British during World War I. When asked the price of remuneration, he replied, "If Britain wins the battle for Palestine, I ask for a national home for my people in their ancient land."[5]

His request resulted in the Balfour Declaration, issued on November 2, 1917. "His Majesty's Government views with favour the establishment in Palestine of a national home for the Jewish people, and will use their best endeavour to facilitate the achievement of this object."[6]

Later in the same month, the British general Sir Edmund Allenby led the charge that gave Great Britain control over Jerusalem. As he was entering the city through the Jaffa Gate, he dismounted his horse and took off his hat, believing that none but the Messiah should enter Jerusalem mounted on a steed.

This intriguing story is reminiscent of many of the battles of Israel in earlier years. General Allenby had ordered planes to fly overhead and leaflets to be dropped, calling the Turks to surrender. These leaflets, signed by Allenby, were taken by the Turkish Muslims to be a directive from Allah for them to leave the city. Not a shot was fired. Ramon Bennett describes the event in his book *When Day and Night Cease* and refers to Isaiah's prophecy: "Like birds flying about, so will the LORD of hosts defend Jerusalem. Defending, He will also deliver it; passing over, He will preserve it" (Isaiah 31:5 NKJV).[7]

Following World War I, in 1920, the League of Nations gave Britain control of "Palestine," but the Balfour Declaration had been forgotten. Fear of Arab reprisals turned British hearts against the Jewish immigrants. Refugees were not allowed to land in the Haifa harbor, and the quota of returning Jews was greatly reduced. Britain installed an Arab government over much of the land that had been biblically promised to Israel.

Another war and a lifetime of horror would transpire before the world's conscience was sufficiently pricked to establish that homeland for the Jews promised by His Majesty. The British government had long since washed its hands of the whole affair. Illegal

Return to the Land

immigrants were sent back to their city of origin or held in detention camps in nearby Cyprus. The fate of the potential Jewish nation now rested in the hands of the United Nations.

A New Nation

The United Nations began to consider the partitioning of "Palestine" to create a homeland for the Jews. A two-thirds majority of the nations was necessary in order for the State to be established.

President Harry Truman's support was essential if the vote was to pass, but he was slow in adding his weight. In fact, the president had been ignoring all requests for a meeting about the partitioning until leaders from the Jewish community contacted Truman's good friend and former business partner, a Jewish man named Eddie Jacobson. Jacobson appealed to the president's sense of history and prevailed upon him to meet with Chaim Weizman, who, though in very poor health, had traveled to the United States and was waiting in a hotel room until the appointment could be secured.

It was this visit with Weizman, the hero of Britain's win in World War I, that strongly influenced Truman's ultimate decision. Without that encounter, the resolution would not have passed. With the president's pressure on several key countries, the vote was taken: 33 nations voted in favor, 13 against, with 10 abstentions. The date was November 29, 1947.[8]

Herzl had spoken prophetically when, in 1897, he predicted that within fifty years the State of Israel would be birthed. Isaiah's words of 2,700 years earlier had become a reality (see Isaiah 66:8). A country was born in a day!

None Left Behind

In spite of the vote, the young nation had to battle seven Arab nations—Egypt, Jordan, Lebanon, Syria, Saudi Arabia, Yemen and

Iraq—to establish itself. Reading about those days is like reading a page from the books of the Kings or Chronicles in the Bible:

> Israel fielded 18,000 men, 10,000 rifles, 3,600 submachine guns, a few old field guns, two tanks, and four planes, of which two were shot down the first day.
>
> Israel was not only hopelessly outnumbered, she did not even possess sufficient guns for each man to have one of his own! Against full-fledged air forces, Israel had next to no air power. And if they had not somehow stolen two tanks from the British, they would have been completely without armour. Nevertheless, by the time the UN managed to arrange a cease-fire between the warring parties, Israel was holding nearly three times the area of land that she had been allocated in the partition![9]

Every Israeli war has seen its miracles. There was a time in the 1967 Sinai campaign when two Israeli tanks topped a sand dune and found themselves facing a complete Egyptian tank unit. With no explanation, the Egyptians stopped, opened their turrets, jumped out and began to flee through the desert. After the Egyptians were captured, they explained their actions, telling stories of the "hundreds of Israeli tanks" they had encountered.[10]

Israel's return to the Land can only be explained as God fulfilling the words of His prophets.

Israel's return to the Land can only be explained as God fulfilling the words of His prophets. At a time when there seemed to be no way for them to go on, the Lord provided a way.

Many of the wars initiated against Israel only ended with an increase in square miles for the fledgling nation. When the new State of Israel was established, the landmass consisted of 3,000 square miles. At the conclusion of the War of Independence in 1948, that had increased to eight thousand square miles. The Six-Day War of 1967 expanded her landmass to 26,000 square miles; the Yom Kippur War of

1973, to 36,000 square miles, though some of this has now been returned. But even this did not yet measure up to Israel's full inheritance as promised to both Abraham and Joshua (see Genesis 15:18; Joshua 1:4).

At the time the State of Israel was formed, Israel's population was less than one million. By 1973, it was still less than three million. Today the total population has reached over eight million, of which over six million are Jewish.[11] In the years of Israel's modern history, her people have returned from over one hundred nations and have endured six major wars and numerous border skirmishes, bombings, rocket attacks and other wartime assaults from their neighbors.

But the story is not complete. There are still twelve million, perhaps more, of Israel's children scattered throughout the nations. Ezekiel speaks of a time when they will all gather to their own land, "not leaving any behind" (39:28). If the prophet's words are to be taken literally—and this is always the assumption until proven otherwise—then every Jew will one day return to the land of Israel.

Similarly, if Paul's words are to be taken literally—and why not?—all Israel will be saved. Does this mean every single Jewish person? Maybe Paul is speaking hyperbolically, but at the very least, it would seem that the Jewish people, someday in history, will be known as those who have acknowledged their Messiah—that the synagogues of the world will become proclaimers of the good news of Yeshua's coming and the anticipation of His return to finish the work. Let us pray toward that end.

After years of ministry, Jewish believers David and Emma Rudolph established Gateways Beyond International, a Messianic missional community committed to sharing a life of daily worship and prayer, discipleship training and world outreach.

123

Remarks from David and Emma Rudolph,
Gateways Beyond International

Emma and I were on a personal retreat in Comparmo, Italy. One Shabbat morning, Cheshvan 10, 5769 (November 8, 2008) was a defining life change for us. As we read and prayed through our morning devotional time, the air became heavy with what could only be called a heavenly Presence. Emma remembered how she had felt a similar Presence twice before when she heard these words: *Go to Israel and put a stake of inheritance into the ground.*

My (David's) first trip to Israel was in the winter of 1979– 1980. We had just returned from our first mission posting in India and had flown to England for some family rest and refreshment. Throughout our travels and ministry in the UK that year, Christian Zionists kept divinely crossing our path with prophetic encouragement: "It's time for your family to be planted in Israel." Over and over, this same theme was repeated by well-meaning folks. Later, I was invited to travel with a new friend for two weeks in the Land of Promise. By the time I returned to our family, I had a personal epiphany to relocate to Israel ASAP.

Two years later, Emma and I traveled together for an exploratory trip. Within the first few days of stepping onto that sacred ground, she encountered her own inner witness to our moving there. Later, back in the United States, our mission ministry blossomed and the plan to emigrate was shelved.

And then, in Comparmo, on that November morning in 2008, we were faced with the same dilemma Abraham must have felt some years after his own personal calling. He had heard clearly from the Lord to leave all: "Get out of your country . . . to a land that I will show you." In his excitement, he shared with his family and his father, Terah, who then led them as far as Haran, where the "old man" died. Once again, the Lord spoke to Abraham: "Go."

Not infrequently, our own natural thinking must give way to God's inner promptings that may require childlike faith. In a word, "our old man has to die" before we can clearly hear and obey. That Hebrew calendar date held a whole new significance as we researched what might have happened that very day in Jewish history. Cheshvan 10 is the date attributed to Noah and his family entering the Ark, though it had not begun yet to rain. They were to mourn for seven days for Noah's grandfather, Methuselah, who had just passed away. Another "old man" died.

For Emma, this was the third time she had heard the Lord speaking to her: *Go . . . put a stake into the ground*. Only this time, she was sobbing uncontrollably, recalling generational shadows that had plagued her past for decades. It was time to step out of that shroud of secrecy, declare her Jewish roots and regain her lost inheritance. Emma was convinced that this time we must not delay.

We arrived in Israel seven days later with our youngest son, Isaac, to put a "stake in the ground." On the last day of our three-week search for a place to live, we received a call from friends to "come quickly and lease the 'perfect' apartment in Jerusalem." Isaac and I literally ran twenty minutes from the office of the lawyer, whom we had just authorized to find a dwelling on our behalf. We had been about to leave for the airport, headed back to Cyprus, where we had been living for the last ten years. By the time we arrived, Emma had already walked through the apartment and had a clear *yes* in her heart. The rest is now history.

From that first journey to Israel—our first step out of exile—until the day we received our citizenship, exactly thirty years had passed before we took up residence in the Promised Land . . . to fulfill yet another call of God on our lives.

9

The Awakening

They will come trembling to the LORD and to his blessings
in the last days.

Hosea 3:5

I did not know their names. In fact, I had never met any of them.
Yet, while driving through the streets of Jerusalem one day, I
prophesied over the people as I passed by. The car windows were
rolled up so that none could hear me, but that was not important.
I was foreseeing a time when many of these people would come to
know Yeshua as Messiah. I have read their Scriptures that speak
of Israel's awakening when they are back in the Land.

Later, I stood before a Jewish congregation in Haifa. Behind
me was the ark that contained the Torah scroll, the handwritten
words of Moses that are read in the synagogues of the world each
Sabbath. Before me were 150 believers in Yeshua, living evidence
that the words of Isaiah are being fulfilled in our day.

"It is a joy to see you with my natural eyes," I said. "For years
I have seen you with my spiritual eyes. I have read about you in

the words of the prophets and the apostles. But now you are here. More of you are coming. I see tens of thousands of family members and friends who will come to faith in the Messiah Yeshua. Who of you would have imagined ten years ago that today you would believe that Yeshua/Jesus is the Messiah of Israel? But the Lord has drawn you. This is the day for your eyes to be opened."[1]

Reuven's Story

Reuven Doron is the grandson of early twentieth-century Russian immigrants to Israel. On foot, one of his grandfathers crossed the mountains of Turkey and eventually wound up in northern Galilee. The other brought his family by ship. Both played significant roles in the founding of the young nation.

At age nineteen, Reuven served in a specialized military unit on the Golan Heights in the Yom Kippur War of 1973. Two-thirds of the men in his unit never made it home. Though Reuven survived the war, he was left with questions for which he had no answers. He was restless, disillusioned and grieved. What was life all about? What meaning could there be to the tragedies he had experienced?

He packed his bags and headed out into the world—Europe, Canada and Central America—before settling in at the Business College of Arizona State University in Phoenix. There he had a life-defining encounter with the God of Israel.

In order to help finance his schooling, Reuven gave private Hebrew lessons. One of his students was a Gentile named Frank. "Why would you, a blond, blue-eyed Gentile, want to learn Hebrew?" Reuven asked him one day.

"Because I've always wanted to be able to read the Scriptures in the original Hebrew language," the man replied. "In the Bible I find the knowledge of the living God."

Reuven never recovered from this candid answer. He had studied the Bible in the schools of Israel, but for him it was merely a book of ancient legends and national myths. God was distant, impersonal and uninvolved with daily life. Now Reuven had to take another look. Could it be that this Book did reveal the living God?

"If there is a God, if He is at all interested in me, if He really paid for my sins, then not only do I want to read about Him and hear of Him, I need to know Him!" Reuven admitted to his student.

"Then go pray. Seek His face," was the advice given.

Reuven accepted the challenge. Night after night he poured out his questions to this faceless God who did not seem to answer.

Yet he knew that one question remained, a question that no Jewish man or woman wants to ask. Could it be that this One whom Christians have worshiped through the ages, this Jewish Man whose followers sometimes turned against Israel—could it be that He was the Promised One?

Reuven felt trapped by his own need to know the truth. Finally, frustrated and angry, he hurled his one remaining question into the night sky: "Do I need Him? Do I need the Nazarene in order to come to You?"

Let Reuven tell you in his own words what happened next.

This time, God answered! Out of heaven came an arrow of revelation, piercing through the darkness of the night, through the world and through my soul. His Word now sparked my spirit alive with a blaze of truth as He spoke, "Yes" and "Amen! You need the Nazarene!"

For the first time in my life, I consciously heard God. The ring of His Word was so clear and loud that, even if the word had come audibly, the sound would have been insignificant compared to the thunder in my spirit! And so I stayed right there, kneeling in my backyard, drinking in the life and nectar of His Word. . . . It was some time before I stood to my feet and returned to my apartment. To my amazement, a most unusual sensation and realization came upon me. I remember saying to myself, "Reuven, you have changed. You need to get reacquainted with yourself." You see,

129

though I had no intellectual knowledge of the new birth doctrine, I simply was spiritually "born again" as the seed of heaven was planted in my heart![2]

Hosea had spoken of Reuven and a host of other Jewish believers living in our time.

> The Israelites will live many days without king or prince, without sacrifice or sacred stones, without ephod or idol. Afterward the Israelites will return and seek the LORD their God and David their king. They will come trembling to the LORD and to his blessings in the last days.
>
> Hosea 3:4–5

No king or prince since 586 BC, when Nebuchadnezzar took Zedekiah to Babylon (see Jeremiah 52:9–11). No sacrifice since the forces of General Titus destroyed the Temple in AD 70. Our day is the "afterward" in which Reuven and hundreds of thousands of other sons and daughters of Jacob have come or will come trembling to the Lord and to His blessings in these last days.

Isaiah's Mandate

Isaiah, too—who had a terrifying encounter with the Holy One, the God of Israel—had foreseen the day in which we live. He heard the angels worshiping around the throne. He felt the doorposts and thresholds of the Temple shake. The air was filled with smoke. Isaiah cried, "I am ruined! For I am a man of unclean lips . . . and my eyes have seen the King, the LORD Almighty" (Isaiah 6:5).

An angel came and touched his mouth with live coals from the altar, saying, "Your guilt is taken away and your sin atoned for" (verse 7).

Then the Lord spoke, "Whom shall I send? And who will go for us?" (verse 8).

"Here am I. Send me," Isaiah blurted out, having no idea of the message he was to deliver to Israel (verse 8).

"Go and tell this people," the Lord said. "'Be ever hearing, but never understanding; be ever seeing, but never perceiving.' Make the heart of this people calloused; make their ears dull and close their eyes. Otherwise they might see with their eyes, hear with their ears, understand with their hearts, and turn and be healed" (verses 9–10).

Jesus used Isaiah's words to explain why Israel as a nation did not receive Him (see Matthew 13:14–15). The apostle John also remembered Isaiah's prophecy when he said, "Even after Jesus had done all these miraculous signs in their presence, they still would not believe in him" (12:37). Indeed, John says, "They could not believe" (12:39). "God gave them a spirit of stupor," adds the apostle Paul, referring back to the same words of Isaiah (Romans 11:8).

"Could not believe"? "Spirit of stupor"? Those are strong terms.

What does this mean? The ways of the Lord are beyond our comprehension. Why would God close Israel's corporate eyes and ears to the very message they were destined to bring to a lost world?

"Because of their transgression, salvation has come to the Gentiles," Paul continues in the same Roman letter (11:11).

Could there have been no other way? Paul is silent. God is silent.

"Their transgression means riches for the world, and their loss means riches for the Gentiles" (verse 12).

"Unfair!" we cry. But there is no answer. Only the testimony of the centuries that Isaiah heard accurately.

How Long?

Isaiah's revelation did not stop with closed eyes and ears and a hardened heart. "For how long, O Lord?" he asked. "How long will this last? How long will their eyes be closed? How long will their hearts be hardened?"

Isaiah had spoken of deserted homes, ruined fields and a forsaken land—words that were fulfilled in detailed accuracy. The Babylonians, Persians, Greeks, Romans, Byzantines, Arabs, Turks, Crusaders and British—each ruled the land before another "Israel" arose.

During those intervening centuries, fields were salted to destroy their fertility. Trees were cut down to avoid the taxation levied against them. Malaria swamps became commonplace.

When Mark Twain visited Israel during the latter part of the nineteenth century, he described it as a land that was utterly desolate. Yet the Jewish people have always been drawn back to this promised inheritance. Through the ages their Passover liturgy—"Next year in Jerusalem!"—has reminded them of their ultimate homeland.

"As the terebinth and oak leave stumps when they are cut down, so the holy seed will be the stump in the land," Isaiah was told (6:13).

The stump would grow again. Israel would return. And when she returned, Isaiah's "until" would be fulfilled: Her eyes and ears would not remain closed, her heart no longer hardened.

Ezekiel's valley of dry bones vision (see Ezekiel 37) parallels Isaiah's vision. Isaiah saw the land devastated, the population gone; Ezekiel saw a valley of dry bones, a nation that no longer existed. Isaiah saw a stump that would grow again; Ezekiel saw the bones come together—the northern and southern kingdoms united, no longer two nations, but one. He saw breath—spiritual life—entering the resurrected nation.

> I will take you out of the nations; I will gather you from all the countries and bring you back into your own land. I will put my Spirit in you and move you to follow my decrees and be careful to keep my laws. *Then [you] will know* that I am the LORD.
>
> Ezekiel 36:24, 27, 38 (emphasis added)

You will know that I am the Lord when the fields are again plowed and sown! You will know that I am the Lord when I multiply

your population again! You will know that I am the Lord when
the towns are inhabited and the ruins rebuilt! You will know that
I am the Lord when the number of men and animals dwelling in
you increase! You will know that I am the Lord when I make you
more prosperous than before!

The Jesus Generation

The year 1967 is the date to remember.

Since the first century, there has never been a generation that
has seen so many Jewish people in so many parts of the world—
both in Israel and in the Diaspora—coming to believe in Jesus.
Something happened in the heavens when Jerusalem came under
Israeli control in 1967.

The June 21, 1971, issue of *Time* magazine carried an extensive article describing the Jesus Movement of the late '60s. Three
times in the article, the writer dates the
beginning of the movement to 1967.[3] It
was during that era that a great majority
of today's leaders in the Messianic Jewish
movement came to faith in Yeshua.

Joseph Shulam, a native Israeli Messianic
leader in Jerusalem, says, "In the early 1960s,
it was difficult to find even two dozen Jews in
Jerusalem who believed in Yeshua the Messiah. Those who were around lived under a
terrible fear of being exposed and totally
ostracized by the Jewish community."[4]

> *Since the first century,
> there has never been
> a generation that has
> seen so many Jewish
> people in so many
> parts of the world
> coming to believe
> in Jesus.*

Now, about fifty years later, there are hundreds in Jerusalem
and multiple thousands throughout the nation who believe that
Yeshua is the Messiah, and there is no longer the same stigma to
being a believer. Unquestionably, Messianic Judaism is by far the
fastest-growing segment of the Jewish community.

Rarely is there a family who has not been affected by the growing number of Jews who have come to faith in Yeshua/Jesus, and an ever-increasing number of Jewish people and Jewish scholars are advocating for greater receptivity within the Jewish community. One of the first Jewish scholars to bring this into discussion was Amy Jill Levine, professor of New Testament at Vanderbilt University in Nashville and an esteemed member of the Jewish community.

Another well-known member of our community, Dr. Frank Boehm, was embarrassed some years ago when his son, Thomas, announced his faith in Jesus. That is no longer the case. Frank and Thomas later became known as the "Boehm Boys," speaking in churches, at civic functions and in the Jewish community, explaining how they had come to love and appreciate each other's stands, even with theological disagreements.

My entire circle of Jewish friends, those who accept Jesus as their Messiah and those who do not, were surprised when the Pew Research Center found that 34 percent of American Jews do not believe that faith in Jesus negates one's Jewishness.[5]

Isaiah's vision is coming to pass. Eyes are opening, sometimes almost involuntarily. Most would prefer that their search for truth *not* end in Jesus. Yet they *do* want truth.

I met Gari when she moved to Nashville from Florida. Her faith in Jesus came after being partially paralyzed for eight and a half years following an automobile accident. Reared in New York, she had gone to the beach, crutches and all, for a time of rehabilitation. A "beach evangelist" began a conversation with her.

"I'm Jewish," she had told him. "We do not believe in Jesus." And yet something in her began to stir. Why was she so annoyed? Did this unexpected encounter touch a need within her?

Later she hobbled into a restaurant and found the only vacant stool at the bar. The man sitting next to her began to dialogue. He told her that he often frequented bars to find people who were in need of an eternal answer to their problems—the answer was Jesus!

After giving her usual "Not interested" reply, she found herself accepting his invitation to attend a church. She was later irritated by her own unaccustomed response, but she was not one to go back on her word.

When she sat down in the church, she could not help but notice the jacket worn by the man beside her. It was a denim jacket with a huge star of David on the back. Inside the star was a Christian symbol. She wept during the entire two-hour assembly.

What is this? she wondered. *Am I being brainwashed? What is happening to my emotions? I'm out of control!*

Back at her mother's home, Gari opened up some of the literature given to her at the church. Among the pamphlets was a brochure telling how to accept the Lord, and it included a sample prayer for inviting Jesus into one's heart. As Gari read the words, she started to pray and then stopped abruptly, astonished at her own reaction. Then, almost carelessly, she added, "Jesus, if You are real, I need to know it."

The bones in her spine began to crack as the longtime paralysis lifted from her body. Even an astigmatism in her eyes, which she had had all her life, was healed!

For fifteen minutes, she paced the floor in wonder, believing herself to have been caught up in some kind of dream. She did not want to leave the room for fear it was all in her imagination. "You *are* real!" she finally declared to the Messiah she had never known.

Gari loves to tell the story. Now she is praying for that sovereign intervention of God in the lives of her family and friends.[6]

Stan Telchin, a Million-Dollar Round Table insurance man, was trying to convince his older daughter that her newfound faith in Yeshua was invalid when he came to faith. He bought Bibles, commentaries and study guides and set out to prove that Jesus was not the Messiah. He went to his rabbi with his questions, looking for a reason not to believe. Stan was so emotionally opposed to his own findings that he could not admit his faith. Not until he heard himself ending a prayer in the name of Yeshua was he aware that faith had arisen in his heart without his conscious permission. His spiritual eyes were opened, just as Isaiah had said they would be!

Stan's wife, Ethel, had a similar experience. "I had gone to bed the night before, still believing that while Jesus was a good man, He was not who He said He was. When I awoke in the morning, I knew it was true. *Jesus is the Messiah.*"[7]

Faith came to Dr. Stephen Stracher, a flight surgeon with the Federal Aviation Administration, while in a Zen meditation hall. He had been told that Jesus and Buddha were saying the same thing, yet he could not harmonize Jesus' agony on the cross with Buddha's relaxation enlightenment.

Pondering the paths of Jesus and Buddha, Stephen realized that, in order to understand how these two paths merged, he would have to experience Jesus fully. But how? Remembering Jesus' claim to be the Messiah of Israel, he knew the answer. To experience Jesus, he must accept Him for who He said He was.

Stephen says, "I said loudly in my mind with complete conviction, *Jesus, I accept You as the Messiah of Israel.* In my mind I heard the words, *The Passover Lamb who takes away the sin of the world.* Without warning or preparation . . . to my utter astonishment I suddenly saw that it was true!"[8]

The revelation of Jesus as Messiah came to Dr. Vera Schlamm while reading from the prophet Isaiah. Vera and her family were freed from the Bergen-Belsen concentration camp following the

Allied victory in February 1945. Becoming a believer in Jesus was the last thing she intended to do, but she was on a serious search for God and was reading from a Bible someone had given her.

"When I came to [Isaiah] 53," she says, "it seemed so obvious that it was talking about Jesus that I thought, *Well, this is a Christian translation, and they have slanted the text to sound that way.* So the following Friday night at the Temple Emmanuel, which I attended regularly, I took the Scriptures from the pew and opened to chapter 53 of Isaiah. The wording was a little different—but it *still* sounded like Jesus!" Only a short time later, Vera confessed her faith in Him.[9]

Much of the Church in this generation has been surprised by the escalation in the number of Israel's children coming to faith. Others have been expecting it.

A few years ago some of our Jewish representatives from the Toward Jerusalem Council II Committee met with two prominent theologians in the Eastern Orthodox Church. After introducing themselves and explaining their mission—to challenge the Church to receive them—our representatives heard the learned men say, "We knew, from our own study of Scripture, that you would be coming. We just did not know that you were already here!"

Do you understand now why I was so confidently praying over my nameless friends in the streets of Jerusalem? Why I know that many of them will yet come to believe? Can you also comprehend why my heart vibrates with joy with each new account of a child of Israel who has come home? Why the prophets' words keep resounding in my spirit?

Centuries ago, long before any of these believers were even born, Hosea, Isaiah, Ezekiel and Paul were seeing Reuven, Gari, Stan and Ethel, Vera, Stephen and thousands more—eyes open, ears listening, hearts softening—receive their King.

Remarks from Norma Sarvis,
Jerusalem, Israel

I was born into an observant, conservative Jewish family, the second generation in the United States. We kept kosher, observed Shabbat, kept the Feasts and lived unto ourselves in a small community in the Deep South.

My overall emotional state as a child was one of total fear—fear of going outside, fear of the non-Jewish world, fear of food that was not kosher, fear of people, fear of life itself. I went through great mental gymnastics just to go to school, but I always felt at home in the nearby synagogue. That was a safe place to me.

When I was a senior in high school, I forced myself to work in a summer camp for handicapped children, forced myself to sleep there, to get outside of myself. The directors captured my attention because they had something I had not seen much of—joy. They talked about God and their Jesus. All this was foreign to me, but I loved their joy.

Once a week, the leaders had a Bible study with the other workers. I did not go since their Bible was not my Bible, and I had always been taught that their God was not my God. So I read a book or watched TV instead. After a few weeks, however, I felt I should at least check it out.

When I reached the room where they were meeting, someone put a Bible in my hands. A very interesting thing began to happen: As one of the leaders read a verse aloud, it sounded to me like another language. I could not understand a single word! And when I tried to read the words on the page, they also appeared scrambled. After a few minutes, I left the room in great frustration, thinking, *Okay, God, this Bible is not for me. They're not even speaking a language that I understand.*

138

Strangely enough, I was drawn to these people and decided to go to church with them one Sunday. When I walked into the small Bible church, again I felt I was in an alien world. I did not understand anything that was going on around me. But when the pastor got up, he began to read Romans 1:16: "For I am not ashamed of the gospel of Christ: for it is the power of God unto salvation to every one that believeth; to the Jew first, and also to the Greek." To my utter amazement, I UNDERSTOOD! All my life, I had been taught that this Book was for the Gentiles, and the Torah was for us Jews. I was totally undone!

Leaving quickly after the service, I walked to my parents' home, which was nearby, went into my room and wept and wept. I thought, *How can this be? Have my parents and rabbis lied to me? Is this Bible of the Gentiles just a fairy tale . . . or the truth? Is this why they have joy—these people?* I pondered that one verse for months, but spoke to no one about it.

In university, I joined a "seekers" group, determined to learn the truth for myself. But when they pulled out the Bible, I still understood not one word. Only the one verse in Romans made any sense to me.

Then one day, someone read these verses: "Do not think that I came to bring peace on earth. I did not come to bring peace but a sword. For I have come to set a man against his father, a daughter against her mother . . . a man's enemies will be those of his own household. He who loves father or mother more than Me is not worthy of Me." I clearly understood that! And I knew this: If the verse in Romans was true, then this was true. And if this was truth, then the verse in Romans was truth. On the basis of these few verses, I decided to give my heart to Yeshua.

I understood only two things: He came for the Jew first . . . and it would cost me everything. Immediately all fear left me.

10

The Resurrected "Nazarenes"

I am a Jew.

Acts 22:3

Not since the demise of the Nazarene communities of the third and fourth centuries have so many of Israel's children come to faith in Yeshua. Jewish believers in those intervening years had been convinced by the Church to give up their own God-given ordinances and feasts to embrace Gentile Christian practices. Those practices were sometimes a coating of Christianity over former pagan customs. The winter equinox celebration, with its trees and Yule log that honored Nordic gods, was translated into Christ Mass, the celebration of the birth of Jesus. Passover became Easter. Circumcision, not required of Gentiles, was replaced by infant baptism and christening. Bar Mitzvah was now confirmation. The Jewish expression of faith in the Jewish Messiah was lost.

This all began to change in 1882, with an influential Jewish leader from Kishinev, Moldova, named Joseph Rabinowitz. Reared in a rabbinical household, Rabinowitz had been ensnared by the skepticism of the Enlightenment. In the face of growing persecution of the Jews in Russia, Rabinowitz had gone to Palestine to consider setting up a colony of returning immigrants. While there, he had a life-changing encounter with the Messiah on the Mount of Olives and went back to his homeland convinced that "Jesus is the King, the Messiah, who alone can save Israel!"[1]

Three years later, in January 1885, the first assemblies of the Israelites of the New Covenant were held. Throngs of people gathered—some out of curiosity, some out of interest, others to cause disturbance. At one point, police officers were posted at the door to keep order. In early February of that year, a street demonstration broke out, threatening Rabinowitz with violence.

All of this did not deter him. In 1890, with the permission of the Russian authorities, Rabinowitz opened the first Messianic synagogue in modern history. Jacob Wechsler, a contemporary of Rabinowitz and a translator of some of his sermons, said, "Who would have believed before that around 100 Israelite men would each Sabbath assemble in a house built in honour of Jesus the Messiah?"[2]

After his Mount of Olives experience, Rabinowitz was absorbed with two subjects—Israel and Yeshua (he always used Jesus' Hebrew name), and he refused to relinquish his Jewish identity. Until his death in 1899, his passport proclaimed him a Jew. On his tombstone, at his express wish, were inscribed these words: "An Israelite who believed in Jehovah and His Anointed, Yeshua of Nazareth, the King of the Jews, Joseph, son of David, Rabinowitz."[3]

Signs of Things to Come

The insistence that he was still Jewish, even though a believer in Yeshua, brought Rabinowitz into continual conflict with both the Church and the Jewish community. Just as in the case of the earlier "Nazarenes," much of the Church did not know what to do with him, and the Jewish community considered him a traitor to the faith of his fathers.

Rabinowitz was very clear in his belief that "through faith alone in Yeshua the Messiah, all men may be justified without the works of the law." Yet he insisted that since "we are the seed of Abraham according to the flesh . . . we are bound to circumcise every male child on the eighth day, as God commanded. And as we are the descendants of those whom the Lord brought out of the land of Egypt with a stretched out arm, we are bound to keep the Sabbath, the feast of unleavened bread, and the feast of weeks, according as it is written in the Law of Moses."[4]

Although the Church as a whole was not comfortable with his unorthodox views, some welcomed Rabinowitz as a firstfruits fulfillment of end-time prophecy. A number of mission boards, influenced by the earlier Puritans' revelation about the Jewish people, were also ready to receive him. Franz Delitzsch, professor of Old Testament at Leipzig, translator of the New Testament into Hebrew and himself a Hebrew Christian, befriended Rabinowitz, as did Alfred Edersheim, the highly respected Jewish Christian theologian.

The synagogue in Kishinev would have been a strange combination for either Jew or non-Jew. Everyone sat bareheaded, and yet there was a menorah. An ark at the front of the hall contained the Torah scroll. The Sabbath text was taken from the portion of Torah for that particular Sabbath, as was the custom in a synagogue. Rabinowitz would often kiss the Torah scroll in Jewish fashion, yet the gospels would also be read.[5]

Support for the new synagogue began arriving from the London Mildmay Mission in England, from the Danish Israel Mission, from churches in Glasgow and Edinburgh, the Swedish Mission and mission groups in Germany. Rabinowitz began to receive more invitations than he could accept. In 1893, he spent over a month in the United States and was invited by Dwight L. Moody, the well-known evangelist, to preach to a Jewish audience at the World Exposition in Chicago.

Rabinowitz was careful to position himself outside of denominational affiliation. He considered the rebirth of the Jewish believing synagogues a resurrection of the early Jewish community, a regrafting of Jewish branches, and felt that this awakening of Israel to faith in their Messiah would "impart the highest life to the dead world," an obvious reference to Romans 11:15.[6]

Peter Hocken, the contemporary Roman Catholic priest and author, recognizes this same need. In his book *The Glory and the Shame*, Hocken writes:

> It is of vital importance for the proper contribution of Messianic Judaism to Christian unity that Gentile Christians, whether Catholic or Protestant, give them the space to develop in fidelity to the Spirit and to make their unique contribution to Catholic-Protestant reconciliation.[7]

In other words, it is important that Jewish believers in Jesus be allowed to find their way to biblically orthodox faith within a modern Jewish expression.

Kai Kjaer-Hansen, Rabinowitz's biographer, sums up the man's life with these words: "The lasting significance of Rabinowitz's activity lies first and foremost in his stubborn insistence that his faith in Jesus had not made him an ex-Jew, and that his Jewish identity had not been drowned in baptism."[8]

Rabinowitz himself compared the Jewish situation to a doctor and his patient. When the doctor is diagnosing the patient's illness, he presses various places on the body, asking such questions as, "Does that hurt? Is this sore? Is there pressure here?" Only when the doctor touches the diseased part of the body does the patient wince in pain.

As long as Rabinowitz spoke disparagingly of the Tanakh, no one flinched. He could even maintain that the writings of Moses were only the writings of a man, not the revelation of God, and the Jewish community was silent. He might even deny God without stirrings. But when he returned to the Holy Land, speaking of Yeshua as the Messiah, he heard screams of pain from all sides.

In spite of the excitement of Jewish mission agencies around the world, Rabinowitz's reestablished Jesus-believing synagogue in Moldova had no permanence. The Russian government's permission for the strange Jewish house of worship was granted only to Rabinowitz personally and died with him. There was no successor. The chapel closed after his death, opening for a brief period before becoming a Greek church and then a cinema. It would appear to be the end of an era.

The Legacy of Joseph Rabinowitz

Yet the memory of Joseph Rabinowitz lingered, fueling the flames of a growing interest in Israel and the Jewish people. Remember that these were also the years of Theodor Herzl and the Zionist Movement, the time when both governments and churches were awakening to a possible rebirth of the Land.

The Hebrew Christian Alliance of America was formed in 1915 "to bring together Jewish believers for fellowship and to be a light to their people."[9] Jewish people began coming to a saving knowledge of Yeshua as Messiah and Savior and joining the mainstream churches in major cities of the United States and England.

In July 1928, the International Hebrew Christian Alliance met in Hamburg, Germany. Sir Leon Levison, the president of the Alliance, mentioned Rabinowitz in his address to the conference. In the summer of 1931, S. H. Wilkinson visited Kishinev and read from the Hebrew Bible, which had been in Rabbi Rabinowitz's possession.

In London, the Mildmay Mission to the Jews, which had supported Rabinowitz, established a Hebrew-Christian congregation. Other such congregations began to spring up with the intention of keeping many of the biblical customs while holding the line that salvation is altogether by grace through faith.

But these were not synagogues such as Rabinowitz had begun. These were missions witnessing to the Jewish people about their Jewish Messiah with the assumption that those who received Him would be a part of an established church.

This was still the thinking at the time of Martin Chernoff's acceptance of his Jewish Messiah in 1940. His wife, Yohanna, tells the story in her book *Born a Jew . . . Die a Jew*.[10] Marty became an ardent disciple of the Lord, sharing his faith passionately with both Jew and Gentile, but assuming that all would join "the Church." For the next thirty years he worked in Jewish missions in the framework of an existing church. Although there were several such Jewish missions, Marty and Yohanna were surprised at the number of Christians who did not believe that a widespread revival was possible until after the rise of the Antichrist and the rapture of the Church. These Christians were not prepared for the unexpected developments of the next few years.

Messianic Judaism Is Born

And then the year that brought a change in the heavenlies. In the late spring of 1967, five surrounding Arab nations began to move their armies and war machinery to Israel's border, intending to destroy the nation. On June 5, Israel launched its preemptive strike and routed those nations in the now-famous Six-Day War. At war's end, Jerusalem, including the Western Wall, the Temple Mount and much of Judea (now called "Palestine territory") and Samaria (now commonly referred to as "the West Bank") were under Israeli control.

About the same time, there began to be a noticeable increase of Jewish believers in Jesus. In the United States, many of those came through the Jesus Movement, which had its beginning in

1967. The need to disciple many of these ardent young believers pushed the Chernoffs toward a major shift in perspective.

The Hebrew Christian Alliance of America conference took place just a few days after the close of the 1967 war. There the Chernoffs sensed change in the air. They were filled with excitement. The retaking of Jerusalem was obviously another sign from heaven, and they were eager to hear what the prophetic teachers and theologians would say.

They found only confusion. Neither Jewish nor Gentile believers knew how to interpret the recent news, and not one conference speaker made reference to it. Martin and Yohanna did not know that many of these scholars had been teaching that Jerusalem would not be back in Israeli control until after the return of the Messiah. They were silent because they had not had time to rearrange their theology!

For the next few years, Marty and Yohanna struggled to hear the heart of God for their young flock. These Jewish believers, like Rabinowitz one hundred years earlier, found no cause to relinquish their Jewishness. They, like the early believers in Acts, were Jews who wanted to worship in Jewish synagogues as followers of Yeshua. There was no such option available.

In early 1970, Marty Chernoff received a visionary directive from the Lord. Two words were emblazoned across the sky in the form of a banner: *Messianic Judaism.* Marty understood that to mean that the time had come to form a body of believers that was not bound to the format of the Church. It was time to open a Jewish synagogue of believers in Jesus.

In October of that year, the Chernoffs resigned from their mission board and incorporated Congregation Beth Messiah in Cincinnati, Ohio. Later they moved to Philadelphia and assumed the leadership of another Messianic congregation, Beth Yeshua, continuing their relationship with the Hebrew Christian Alliance. In 1975, the name was changed to the Messianic Jewish Alliance of America, with Beth Yeshua as one of the visionary congregations on the forefront of the movement.

Historian David Rausch says, "The name change . . . signified far more than a semantical expression—it represented an evolution in the thought processes and religious and philosophical outlook toward a more fervent expression of Jewish identity."[11]

There were similar stirrings in other Jewish hearts. Marty Waldman described his own feelings about being a Jew in a Gentile church when he came to faith in the mid-'70s:

> Although I was generally welcomed into the Church, I soon discovered that my desire to remain identifiably Jewish in my faith was not only discouraged, but oftentimes brought confusion and even accusations of "judaizing." As a new Jewish follower of Jesus, I was experiencing an identity crisis that would not go away.[12]

Today Marty is the spiritual leader of Baruch HaShem, a Messianic synagogue in Dallas, Texas.

Daniel Juster, who came to faith in a Dutch Reformed church and was ordained in a Presbyterian church, began to be drawn back into his own Jewishness and became the founding president of the Union of Messianic Jewish Congregations in the late '70s. Juster would later help to begin the *Tikkun* (restoration) network that oversees congregations in the United States.

None of this existed before 1967, the year the Lord turned that prophetic key in the heavens to unlock some of the hearts of His covenant people.

Fall of Communism—Rise of Evangelism

Messianic Judaism of the 1980s necessarily concerned itself with developing a full-orbed Jewish expression of faith in Yeshua. Weddings, Bar Mitzvahs, day schools, *yeshivot*—to train Messianic rabbis—all emerged. Yet one vital element of the original first-century Messianic community was still lacking—apostolic outreach.

In the early '90s, after the fall of Communism, an amazing spiritual hunger surfaced in Eastern Europe, and that region became a ripe field for harvest. Enter Jonathan Bernis, now president and CEO of Jewish Voice Ministries International. Bernis gained a vision for taking the Gospel to these Eastern European children of Israel, many of whom had forsaken their Jewish identity after generations of persecution and the atheistic indoctrination of Communism. His organization began sponsoring Jewish cultural festivals, always honoring Holocaust survivors, many of whom have received the Messiah. "Since our first festival in '93," he reported in the late '90s, "over 125,000 Russian Jews have made professions of faith in Messiah."[13]

Today Messianic congregations are flourishing in Canada, Western Europe, South America, New Zealand and Australia, and many other places in the world. These congregations bring together Jews and Gentiles in their common faith. Churches in Asia and Africa are awakening to God's irrevocable call on Israel and are restoring their own Jewish roots. According to one of my friends who has spent his life among the Arabs, even among these sons of Ishmael, there is a growing recognition that "salvation is from the Jews" (John 4:22).

In Jesus-believing synagogues, there are not only Jewish believers but there are a number of covenant Gentile partners who are connecting to their own Jewish roots—a foreshadowing of the future.

At the close of the last century, Kai Kjaer-Hansen and Bodil F. Skjott published their *Facts and Myths about the Messianic Congregations in Israel*.[14] At the time, they listed 81 congregations and home groups meeting throughout Israel. According to the latest estimates, there are fifteen to twenty thousand believers meeting in approximately 150 home gatherings or congregations.[15]

In 1967, there were no Messianic Jewish congregations in the world. Today there are hundreds. In the late nineties, according to an article in *Christianity Today*, there were already over 350.[16]

In 1967, there were an estimated two thousand Jewish believers in Jesus worldwide. Today there are hundreds of thousands among the Jewish people. An article in *Charisma* magazine mentions a 1990 survey that suggested that more than one million Jewish people in the United States alone express "some sort of faith in Yeshua."[17]

It is no longer unusual to meet Jewish people who have accepted Jesus as Messiah. Many of these are still a part of the Church in its non-Jewish expression. Some have remained in their local synagogues. Others have formed synagogues where both Jews and non-Jews meet together as partners in this Jew-Gentile connection predicted by the Prophets.

Inside Israel, things are also changing. When I first began visiting Israel, I hesitated to speak to customs officials about my relationship with leaders of Yeshua-believing congregations, lest they be targeted for greater persecution. Today there is an openness to speak freely about faith, even though there are still pockets of persecution.

One of our young Israeli friends was a finalist in Israel's equivalent to *American Idol*. In her interview, she mentioned that she is a follower of Yeshua. This hit a nerve among believers in the Land, so that social media was barraged with others who gratefully proclaimed, *"Gam ani!"* ("I, too!") "I, too, am a believer in Yeshua."

Another of our friends who leads a congregation in Israel was rejoicing recently that, in one day, he baptized 25 new believers into the name of Yeshua, proclaiming their faith with joy.

Our own Caleb Company students,[18] young men and women who do not speak Hebrew and who are in the Land for only a month, are finding that even among Orthodox Jewish men and women, there is often a curiosity to know more about their faith in Jesus.

Growth in the Midst of Opposition

This new profile has emerged despite sometimes fierce opposition. During the early days of Philadelphia's Beth Yeshua, there were bomb threats and death threats. Tires were punctured. Children were spat upon. The Jewish community was irate that a Messianic synagogue was about to buy property in their community. Billboards warned of this "cult" in "your neighborhood" and of the need to "guard your children."[19]

A parade of protest was planned for a Sunday morning. Busloads of participants arrived from other cities. Members of Beth Yeshua turned the intended threat into a celebration of Jewish music and dance and a proclamation of the Jewish Messiah.

Not all that long ago in Dallas, Texas, the Baruch HaShem congregation was gathering for the Sabbath morning worship when a machine gun–wielding neo-Nazi invaded their quiet surroundings. The fact that no one was killed can be credited only to the Lord. Twice the man aimed his gun and pulled the trigger, only to have the gun mysteriously raised to fire harmlessly into the empty skies. Mothers and children froze in fear; some were wounded as they crawled through windows to escape the shooting spree before police arrived and subdued the man. He was later convicted and is spending several years behind bars.

In the former Soviet bloc, the opposition has also been fierce. One Messianic Jewish festival and conference had to be canceled because the police could not ensure protection for those attending. At other events, large halls were emptied mid-performance because of repeated bomb threats.

Resistance to the Messianic movement in Israel has also been strong at times. Returning believing immigrants have sometimes been denied citizenship on the basis of their faith. *Sabra*—native-born Israelis—and other believers have often been persecuted, houses and synagogues vandalized. In one incident the congregation was surrounded while the Sabbath worship was in progress. The worshipers could not leave until police protection was secured. In more recent years, one of the Messianic congregations had attracted such attention because of their humanitarian work in the area, that the *Yad L'Achim* anti-missionaries launched an attack against the worshipers, lining the sidewalks outside their meeting place, spitting on them and cursing them.

The whole scenario is often reminiscent of those early centuries, but the "Nazarenes" are back—this time to stay!

A New Thing

As these synagogues are formed, there have been many questions. The Rabinowitz model is over one hundred years old, and Rabinowitz himself did not have all the answers.

What part of Jewish heritage should be maintained and what part relinquished? What should be incorporated into the new synagogues? What expressions of Jewishness are valid, and which run at cross-purposes to newly acquired faith?

Must there be a Torah scroll? Should the congregations read weekly from those scrolls? Should the meetings be held on the Sabbath? What kind of worship music should be used? Should dance be introduced into worship? Should men wear a *yarmulke*—a small head covering? A *tallith*—Jewish prayer shawl? What form of government? Should the synagogue leaders be called rabbis? How much, if any, Jewish liturgy?

How much should be received from the (Gentile) Church without giving up Jewish identity? What should be done about Gentiles who want to join the movement? Should they be considered for leadership? What can be done to maintain Jewish identity if Gentiles do join? How can Jews unite with the Gentile Church and yet still remain Jewish?

Dan Juster, in his book *Jewish Roots,* writes:

> Sometimes Messianic Jews, in seeking to recapture their Jewish roots, become enamored of Rabbinic customs and Rabbinic worship. I have become convinced that Rabbinic Judaism is a more severe departure from biblical faith than I had ever realized in my early days of Jewish recovery. . . . The atmosphere of the New

Testament carried on the spirit of the Hebrew Scriptures pervasively and profoundly. The essence of Rabbinism is a severe departure, replacing revelation with human reason. . . . We who are Jewish are biblical New Covenant Jews, not Rabbinic Jews![20]

Juster believes that this newly resurrected community is to encourage more creatively produced materials that reflect the fullness of faith in the context of Jewish life and usage. These areas include Jewish dance, food, Hanukkah celebrations, Purim plays, Bar and Bat Mitzvahs (the celebration of young manhood at age thirteen; young womanhood, often at twelve), marrying under a *chupah*—the canopy used for the bridal party during the wedding ceremony—all valid expressions of Yeshua-affirming, Torah-honoring Jewish faith. Torah and Haftorah reading—readings from the Prophets and the historical books—on the Sabbath also keep the connection to the larger Jewish community.

There are all kinds of gatherings designed to bring Jewish believers together, along with non-Jews who appreciate what is happening. Jonathan Bernis and Jewish Voice Ministries International have invited the diverse Jewish ministries together for fellowship—Jews for Jesus, Chosen People, Union of Messianic Jewish Congregations, Messianic Jewish Alliance of America, Tikkun and many others. Another recently formed organization calls itself *FIRM*—Fellowship of Israel Related Ministries, with an intention to "cultivate Messiah-centered relationships that bless the inhabitants of Israel—Jews, Arabs and others—and the Jewish community around the world."[21]

The Church, too, continues to assess this resurrected community. Rick Joyner, author and publisher of *Morning Star Journal*, wrote that he was at first disturbed by the determination of some in the Messianic movement to maintain some degree of separateness from the Church. Later, he began to believe that distancing had been essential.

As it has been widely taught, there are three basic levels to relationships. The first level is codependence. The next level is independence.

The final, and highest, level of relationship for which we need to strive, is interdependence.

On the level of codependence, the weaker personality is usually swallowed up in the stronger one. Because of this, a person usually must go through the phase of independence when they find their identity and become secure in it before they can go to the highest level—interdependence. For this reason the Messianic movement needed to remain independent from the Church until its identity was established. Its identity must be strong enough for a relationship with the Church in which it will not be swallowed.[22]

Even among those who are very affirming of the Jewish believing movement, there is still much to learn and to ponder. Revelation settled a bit deeper to one of my Roman Catholic–reared young brothers when he realized, "Mother Mary was Jewish!"

The return of so many Jewish people to the Messiah in our day reaffirms God's covenant love for His people. We are living out the fulfillment of Isaiah's vision when Jewish eyes would open. We are experiencing what Hosea predicted—Israel coming "trembling to the LORD" (Hosea 3:5). We are watching the breath blown into the resurrected body of which Ezekiel spoke. Paul's words concerning the regrafting are taking on more weight. And we are pondering anew the words of Jesus from that day overlooking the Temple, "When these things begin to take place . . . your redemption is drawing near" (Luke 21:28).

The Lord refuses to close the curtain of history without His beloved Israel.

A recent issue of *Charisma* magazine interviewed and told the story of some of the Messianic leaders in the Land of Israel, but the editors were not fully attuned to the heart of these leaders. On the cover was the stunning headline "These Brave Christians Are Sharing the Love of Jesus in Israel."

My friend Eitan Shishkoff appreciated the special attention given, but responded with an article published by *Charisma* in a later edition. His response was entitled "I Love Jesus, But Don't Call Me Christian!"[23]

Remarks from Eitan Shishkoff,
Tents of Mercy, Kiryat Yam, Israel

I know that the term "brave Christians" was meant as a serious compliment, but it simply is not our self-understanding. We have not converted to Christianity. We have returned to the God of Abraham, Isaac and Jacob through His Messiah, Yeshua. . . . This "turning Jews into Christians" is patently not our aim. . . .

We are seeking with all our hearts to introduce our people to Yeshua, the Messiah promised by the prophets. We are rejoicing in the fulfillment of Jeremiah's prophecy that God would make a new covenant with us. We are growing new houses of worship—not as missionary churches, but as indigenous, Hebrew-speaking, Yeshua-centered congregations in Israel. . . . We want to be known as those who have come home. We've rejoined the nation of the patriarchs and the apostles.

Like Yeshua's first disciples, we see ourselves as those who have neither rejected their heritage nor converted to another religion. We are called by God to identify ourselves as New Covenant Jews, heralding the return of our King. . . . At the same time, we delight in the true brotherhood shared by all His followers, Jew and non-Jew. We are one in the Spirit and sincerely covet your friendship and prayers.

11

Jew and Gentile—
"One New Man"

> His purpose was to create in himself one new man out
> of the two.
>
> Ephesians 2:15

"I'm confused! Is Yeshua not a Jewish Messiah? Is this not my own heritage? Shouldn't the Church be affirming their Jewish roots rather than requiring me to become more like a non-Jew? Is it wrong for me to want the Church to understand?"

In a home gathering of Jewish and Gentile believers, these questions were voiced by a woman who had recently moved to our city from Israel. She was having difficulty finding her place among the community of believers.

I remembered the story of David and Martha Stern, a Jewish couple who are part of a Messianic congregation in Jerusalem. In a conversation with the pastor of a large American church, the pastor spoke of a Messianic leader whom he greatly admired.

"But why does he have to be so Jewish?" he exclaimed. To which Martha Stern responded reflexively, "Why do *you* have to be so Gentile?"

The Church has become a Gentile-Moabitish expression of faith in the Messiah. Still, we consider our churches to be culturally neutral and wonder why Jewish believers would not feel welcome among us, not knowing how far removed we are from the family that birthed us. When we read Paul's Ephesian letter and hear him speaking of Jew and Gentile as "one new man" (2:15), we assume that this one new man will look like "regular church" with Jewish believers added to the mix. Jewish believers, on the other hand, often wonder how the Church can be so insensitive to the very people out of whose loins they were birthed.

Honoring Jewish Heritage

Even though there was no requirement made of the early Gentile believers to become Jewish, it was necessary for them to learn of their Jewish roots and heritage in order to understand faith in Messiah. These early Gentile believers had only the Jewish Scriptures and were, therefore, being taught from the Tanakh—the Hebrew Scriptures. Most of the apostolic writings—New Testament—were not yet available to these early Gentile believers. Only gradually did these writings gain in authority to become a part of the canon of biblical Scripture.

The entire New Testament, much of it written for a Gentile audience, is rooted in the Tanakh. The New Testament can only be fully understood through the lens of Jewish history and the Prophets. Jesus is the Suffering Servant and the Lamb of God. Jewish genealogy is the heritage of both Jew and Gentile. The Genesis account, the Flood, the tower of Babel, the call of Abraham, the sacrifice of Isaac, the Israelites' deliverance from Egypt, the establishment of the kingdom of Israel, the proclamations and predictions of the Prophets, the anticipation of the Anointed One—all form the backdrop from which all history is perceived.

This early "one new man" of which Paul spoke was the coming together of Torah-observant Jewish believers in Yeshua with Gentiles, who though never required to keep the Law, were nonetheless becoming well-grounded in *their* Jewish past.

Paul's letter to the Romans is especially useful as we consider the "one new man." The "visitors from Rome" (Acts 2:10) present on Pentecost morning would have carried the good news about Jesus back to their hometown. Eventually, Gentiles joined them as believers in their Jewish Messiah, who was also the Redeemer of the nations, but the Jewish disciples would have maintained leadership in the community. They were the ones acquainted with Scripture and would, therefore, have been the teachers.

But in a very few years, things changed. The Jews were expelled from Rome during the reign of Emperor Claudius in AD 49 (see Acts 18:2).

Paul wrote his letter as the Jewish people were being allowed back into Rome, but this return presented a problem. Leadership in that short time had become relegated to the Gentiles, but the Jews were back.

From the beginning to the end of Paul's letter to the Romans, he is challenging the attitudes of both Jews and non-Jews. And lest we forget, may I repeat? The Gentiles should never forget:

- Jesus "as to his human nature was a descendant of David" (1:3).

- The Gospel was "first for the Jew, then for the Gentile" (1:16).

- The Jewish people had "been entrusted with the very words of God" (3:2).

- "Theirs [the Jewish people] is the adoption as sons; theirs the divine glory, the covenants, the receiving of the law, the temple worship and the promises" (9:4).

159

- God has not rejected "his people" (11:1).
- They have not stumbled "so as to fall beyond recovery" (11:11).
- Gentiles should make Jewish non-believers "envious [for their own Messiah]" (11:11).
- The Gentiles have now been grafted into a "cultivated olive tree" (11:24).
- They [Gentiles] should not be "arrogant" or "conceited" (11:20, 25) in their relationship with their Jewish brothers and sisters.
- At some future time in history when the "full number of the Gentiles has come in" (11:25), "all Israel will be saved" (11:26).

Paul's later letter to the Ephesians has this same theme. The non-Jews are "no longer foreigners and aliens, but fellow citizens with God's people" (2:19), "heirs together with Israel" (3:6).

Fellow citizens with God's people? Heirs together with Israel? The Gentiles "once were far away" but had been "brought near through the blood of [Messiah]" (Ephesians 2:13). They were reconciled to God and to each other, where both have "access to the Father by one Spirit" (verse 18).

Ruth (the Gentiles) had not replaced Boaz (the Jewish people), only joined him—become a member of his family, a citizen of his Land and partaker of his promises. She had come from a land of famine and been welcomed into the house of abundance. She is now an heir *together with* Boaz, not an heir *in place of* him. She was at one time a foreigner to the covenants of the promise that were his; now she is a sharer together with those promises. She must be careful to "no longer live as the Gentiles do" (Ephesians 4:17).

In the Ephesian letter, there is a certain implied knowledge of the Hebrew Scriptures. This knowledge was resident in these former Artemis worshipers because of Paul's earlier visit to the city, a visit that lasted over two years (see Acts 19:1–20).

This is a new day in relationships between Jewish and Gentile believers. Many of us from the nations no longer wish to be robbed of our biblical heritage. Some of us are celebrating the feasts with our Jewish brothers and sisters. Some are even restoring a true Sabbath rest, a day in which we do nothing that feels like work, a day devoted to the Lord and to our families. Not a legalistic burden, but the joy of ceasing from labor so that we can get fresh strength and anointing for the following week.

Others of us are choosing biblically kosher eating, not because we are under any kind of command to do so, but because we have come to believe that God is the world's best nutritionist, knowing what is best for the bodies He created.

Jordan Rubin spent thousands of dollars seeking healing from Crohn's disease, only to find his healing by returning to the diet of his forefathers. He presents a compelling testimony in his book *The Maker's Diet*.

Return to Unity

In those early congregations, Jew and Gentile lived together in love and unity. True, there is "neither Jew nor Greek," as Paul told the Galatians (3:28), yet that does not eradicate their distinctiveness. No "male nor female," Paul added in the same passage, but who would ever question the uniqueness of each?

The fact that salvation comes through the Jews—that it is to be preached "first to the Jew"—need not be an affront to any people. Israel's surrounding Arab nations, for example, who have found it difficult to acknowledge her identity, will enter the fullness of their intended destiny only as they recognize Israel's Messiah and her claim to the Land deeded to her by God. Ezekiel spoke specifically about a time when "aliens"—those who are not descendants of the twelve sons of Jacob—will be considered "native-born Israelites," in line for an inheritance along with the tribes of Israel (see Ezekiel 47:22), but only as they honor, even join, this chosen family of God.

Isaiah foresees a time when non-Jews will be appointed as priests and Levites (see Isaiah 66:18–21). Non-Jews enter their full inheritance only as they recognize and submit to the Jewish Messiah.

For a brief moment in history, there existed a fascinating blend of Jew and Gentile as Jewish apostles preached the good news to the nations in the early first century. That unique blend began to be marred as Gentiles kept Jewish Scripture, but renounced much of their Jewish legacy. Their oneness was further damaged when the Church began to demand that Jewish believers forsake their own God-ordained, fulfilled-in-Messiah customs and feasts and join in the often-rooted-in-paganism Gentile culture. Jesus' reference to the "times of the Gentiles" was now understandable.

The Times of the Gentiles

Both Jesus and Paul imply that Gentile dominance would end: Jesus spoke of the "times of the Gentiles" being fulfilled (Luke 21:24); Paul said "the full number of the Gentiles" would "come in" before the change would occur (Romans 11:25). Paul obviously did not mean there would be no more Gentiles coming to faith, since he had just referred to the great revival that would break out when Israel began to receive Messiah (see verse 12). What did Paul mean? To what did Jesus refer?

The history of Israel, from the call of Abraham to the baptism of Cornelius, had been the "times of the Jews." Although there were occasions when God revealed Himself to people other than Abraham and his sons of the promise, the most consistent and clearest revelations were reserved for this covenant family. Only they were given prophetic insights into man's future redemption through a messiah. This "time of the Jews" continued during the time of Jesus' ministry and during the early days following His ascension.

Cornelius's miraculous welcome into this otherwise Jewish family began a rapid transition. We entered into a brief "Jew-Gentile" season in which the Jewish people were generally still in leadership, but Gentile believers were rapidly coming to the forefront of the faith movement.

Within a few years, the leadership had changed, and for the next nineteen centuries, we entered into the "times of the Gentiles." Amazingly, Jewish tradition speaks of two thousand years before Torah, two thousand years of Torah and two thousand years of the Gentiles. Then the Messiah is to come and usher in a "sabbatical" seventh millennium.

Today the scene has changed again. The Jews are back among the community of believers. We are in another Jew-Gentile season. Unfortunately, much of the Church is unaware of the gravity of this change. Prophecies that have lain dormant for centuries are being fulfilled.

Thankfully, a growing number of the Church has recognized the significance of the change and are welcoming the Jewish believers back. Gentiles are taking upon themselves the sins of the past and openly repenting of their anti-Jewish bias through the centuries.

We are about to see Jewish leadership restored to the entire Body of the Lord. We are entering a time when the Jewish nation will become known as worshipers of Jesus/Yeshua, and the whole Church will honor and accept Israel's fulfilled role as a light to

We are about to see Jewish leadership restored to the entire Body of the Lord.

the nations (see Isaiah 60:3). If that statement seems far-fetched, consider that the events of the last fifty years would have been deemed impossible a generation ago!

It could be a combined Jew-Gentile leadership that we are to expect. First, in the time of the Jews, the leadership was Jewish.

Then came the time of the Gentiles. But we will see the coming together of a Jew-Gentile Bride before the Lord's return.

The transition from Jewish to Gentile leadership required several decades. The transition to a Jew-Gentile leadership is still in its initial stages, and we cannot be sure what form it will take. One thing is certain: Jewish believers are here to stay. Another is equally certain: Jewish leadership in the whole Body of the Lord is rising again. Furthermore, Jerusalem, Israel and the Jewish people are moving again into the prophecy-fulfilling stage of world history, and we will ultimately see a Jewish Man ruling over the entire world. The title of Joel Richardson's book *When a Jew Rules the World*[1] may have been provocative, but it does indeed proclaim the future of our planet.

Future Role of Jerusalem and Israel

It was to Israel and Israel's Messiah that God said through Isaiah: "Arise, shine, for your light has come. Nations will come to your light" (60:1, 3). That prophecy was only partially fulfilled in earlier centuries. Israel's full destiny has yet to be realized. An international revival of praise and righteousness is still ahead (see 61:11). God's calendar of new moons and Sabbaths will take on renewed meaning for all mankind (see 66:23). Jesus Himself will eat the Passover in the fulfilled kingdom of God (see Luke 22:16).

Jerusalem, Zion and Israel will be the esteemed names of an honored people, as former oppressors bow at their feet, calling them "the City of the LORD, Zion of the Holy One of Israel" (Isaiah 60:14). Jerusalem will be a "crown of splendor in the LORD's hand" (62:3). This is why Isaiah will not remain silent until he sees righteousness shining out and salvation blazing forth from this favored city (see 60:1–2).

With the prophet Isaiah, we yearn for that time when "the earth will be full of the knowledge of the LORD as the waters cover the sea" (11:9), when all Israel will "be righteous and they will possess the land forever" (60:21).

With Jeremiah, we agree that "Judah will be saved and Jerusalem will live in safety" (33:16).

We pray and we wait. We wait for His [Messiah's] feet to "stand on the Mount of Olives," for the mountain to be "split in two" (there is a geological fault line at just the right place) and for the Lord to reign as "king over the whole earth" (Zechariah 14:4–5, 9).

We look for the time when children live out their intended life spans; when wolf and lamb, lion and calf, lie down together; when "the infant will play near the hole of the cobra," and there will be neither harm nor destruction "on all my holy mountain" (Isaiah 11:6–9; 65:20, 25).

We pray, we wait and we hope.

"Lord, are you at this time going to restore the kingdom to Israel?" the disciples inquired following Jesus' resurrection and shortly before His ascension (Acts 1:6).

"It is not for you to know the times or dates the Father has set by his own authority," was Jesus' reply (verse 7). In other words, "You have accurately read the Prophets. There will be a restoration of the kingdom to Israel. Your thinking is correct, but the timing is not for you to know."

Jesus must remain in heaven until time for everything to be restored "as he promised long ago through his holy prophets," Peter told his listeners a few days later (Acts 3:21).

How do we act in this interim as we await the ultimate fulfillment? What does this "one new man" look like in these early days of the twenty-first century?

We will see a return to that which was begun in the first century. Jewish believers remain Jewish in practice, often in their own synagogues, as Gentile congregations are restored to an appreciation of their Jewish heritage.

As we revive that first-century model, more and more Messianic Jewish synagogues will arise. Gentiles will choose to be a part of those congregations as they grow in love for the Jewish people and reclaim their lost Jewish roots. Daily Bible readers will refrain from mentally substituting the word "Church" when reading "Israel" and will receive God's heart of compassion for His covenant people and their role in world redemption. The biblical calendar will take on new significance as the redeemed from all nations will see the imprint of God in these fulfilled and being-fulfilled-in-Messiah annual reminders. These Gentile believers will delight in joining their Jewish brothers and sisters in proclaiming God through the biblical feasts. They will want to express their love for the God of Abraham, Isaac and Jacob in practices He ordained.

At the same time, the heart of the Church will begin to be turned in love for Jerusalem, for Israel and for all Jewish people everywhere. Mission efforts around the world will begin to remember Paul's "first-to-the-Jew" admonitions to the Romans. Pastors who are preaching in an expository way through the book of Romans will no longer ignore chapters 9 through 11 as if they were an interruption in an otherwise excellent epistle. Church choirs will be rehearsing their Christmas specials and begin to weep as new revelation opens their hearts to the literal meaning of the words they are singing:

> O come, O come, Emmanuel, and ransom captive Israel!
> Rejoice, rejoice, Emmanuel will come to you, O Israel![2]

Jesus Himself was an expression of the One New Man through His natural bloodline. He was not only a son of Abraham, Isaac and Jacob, but also of Rahab and Ruth. Yet He lived out His life in fulfillment of the prophets and promises, and will return as the Lion of the Tribe of Judah.

Remarks from Joan Masterson,
One in Messiah Ministry, New Providence, New Jersey

I am a Jewish believer brought to faith by a loving Gentile and completely assimilated into the Church for almost forty years. A visionary encounter with Yeshua changed my direction to find out what it meant to be a Jew in the body of Messiah. I have walked out this new journey, having come to an understanding that yes, as a Jew, I am to maintain my Jewishness, not by holding on to all our traditions, but as one who walks in God's ways, guided by His Holy Spirit.

What does it mean to be a son or daughter adopted into the household of faith? "You are all sons of God through trusting in Messiah Yeshua. There is neither Jew nor Greek . . . there is neither male nor female—for you are all one in Messiah Yeshua," Paul told the Galatians. "And if you belong to Messiah, then you are Abraham's seed—heirs according to the promise" (3:26–29 TLV).

Does this mean we lose identity as man and woman or as Jew and Gentile? No. A child adopted from a foreign nation never loses his or her ethnicity, though the child takes on the identity and values of the new household. So what will this new Jew-Gentile body of Yeshua look like? Will it look Jewish? I would rather like to think that it will look biblical without all the rabbinic explanations, Church theology or mixture of pagan cultures.

I am a daughter of the household of faith in Yeshua. I am an heir "according to the promise."

A Time to Pray

You who call on the LORD, give yourselves no rest, and give
him no rest till he establishes Jerusalem and makes her the
praise of the earth.

Isaiah 62:6–7

The year is 522 BC. Daniel, having lived in Babylon for almost as
long as he can remember, is now an old man. One day, while reading from the Jeremiah scroll, he is held captive by the prophet's
clear prediction: "When seventy years are completed for Babylon,
I will . . . bring you back to this place" (29:10).

It's true, Daniel thought, as he remembered the years since his
own deportation to Babylon under Nebuchadnezzar. Five other
kings had reigned in Babylon before its fall to Persia. Then a new
king by the name of Cyrus ascended Persia's throne.

Anticipation was high among the exiles in Babylon when Cyrus
became king. Isaiah had called this man by name almost two centuries before his birth, predicting that he would issue a decree to
free the exiles and begin the rebuilding of the city and the Temple

169

(see Isaiah 44:28 and 45:13). It happened exactly as Isaiah had foreseen that Cyrus would decree: "Let [Jerusalem] be rebuilt. . . . Let [the Temple's] foundations be laid" (cf. Ezra 5:13).

The work on the city and the Temple began with great exuberance. But King Cyrus died before the work was completed, and Persia's next king was not so favorably disposed toward these sons of Israel.

It is the first year of King Darius's reign as Daniel is again reading the familiar words. "Seventy years," he muses as he reads from Jeremiah. "It has been seventy years since the Temple was destroyed. The full number of the years is fast approaching. The fullness of the time has come. HaShem's (Hebrew for 'The Name') Word never fails. We must continue in prayer until we see its completion."

Daniel lays aside the scroll and begins to pray:

> O LORD, the great and awesome God, who keeps his covenant of love with all who love him and obey his commands, we have sinned and done wrong. We have been wicked and have rebelled; we have turned away from your commands and laws. We have not listened to your servants the prophets. . . .
>
> Lord, you are righteous, but this day we are covered with shame . . . because of our unfaithfulness to you. O LORD, we and our kings, our princes and our fathers are covered with shame because we have sinned against you. . . .
>
> Now, our God, hear the prayers and petitions of your servant. . . . O LORD, hear and act! For your sake, O my God, do not delay (Daniel 9:4–19).

As Daniel knelt in prayer, he was carrying upon his shoulders the sins of generations—from Judah and all Israel, those in the land and those in exile, kings and princes. He confessed sins for which he was not personally responsible, but whose tragic consequences had shaped his life.

King Darius needs to read this, Daniel may have thought. *He needs to know that his own grandfather Cyrus was named as*

Israel's benefactor over two hundred years ago. He needs to see Jeremiah's prediction of the return.

The scene is imagined, but the facts are true. It was in the first year of Cyrus's reign that Jeremiah's prophecy began to be fulfilled (see Ezra 1:1). It was in the sixth year of Darius's reign when the Temple was completed (see 6:15).

By that time, Ezra and Nehemiah had returned to Jerusalem with "Daniel prayers" on their own lips. "O my God, I am too ashamed and disgraced to lift up my face to you . . . our sins are higher than our heads. . . . From the days of our forefathers until now, our guilt has been great," Ezra agonizes as he intercedes before God (9:6–7).

"I confess the sins we Israelites, including myself and my father's house, have committed against you. We have acted very wickedly toward you," Nehemiah laments (1:6–7), as this civil governor agrees with the prayers of Ezra the priest.

Partners with God

From the reading of Scripture as well as interpreting the times, Daniel, Ezra and Nehemiah knew of God's intentions for their day. They also understood that they could partner with the Lord to help bring about its completion. Daniel's partnership was primarily in prayer and fasting (see 9:2–3). Ezra and Nehemiah, who returned to the Land, led the people in repentance and in the rebuilding of the wall.

> *We have seen a partial fulfillment of God's will regarding Israel, her coming to faith and the world revival. Our role is to give ourselves to intercession, confessing the sins of our fathers and rulers until we see the work completed.*

Our position today is precisely the same as Daniel's in his day. We have seen a partial fulfillment of God's will regarding Israel, her coming to faith and the world revival. Our role, like Daniel's, is to give ourselves to intercession, confessing the sins of our fathers and rulers until we see the work completed.

God is looking for those who will join Him in His work. "I looked for a man among them who would . . . stand before me in the gap on behalf of the land," He told Ezekiel (22:30). "Whatever you bind on earth will be bound in heaven," Jesus told His disciples, obviously not to affirm their selfish desires but in order to release His plans upon the earth. "If two of you on earth agree about anything you ask for, it will be done" (Matthew 18:18–19).

In John's vision of heaven, the work of God could not be released upon the earth until the bowls of incense, containing the prayers of the saints, were filled (see Revelation 5:8; 8:3–5). Paul assures us that the promises of God will all be fulfilled. Yet the "Amen" is to be spoken by us (see 2 Corinthians 1:20).

Strange. There are plans of God that will not go into effect until we first pray to know His will and then pray for it to be done. It is out of this understanding that Isaiah cried, "Give yourselves no rest, and give him no rest till he establishes Jerusalem and makes her the praise of the earth" (62:6–7).

Daniel read Jeremiah and would not rest until he saw the fulfillment of what he had read. Ezra and Nehemiah understood the intentions of the Lord in their day and could not rest until it was accomplished.

I am a Daniel! I am an Ezra! I am a Nehemiah!

I am Don! I have seen the sins of my people! They are mine to confess and mine to renounce. It is my role to intercede, to stand in the gap, to ask for mercy for us all. I understand some of the Lord's intentions for our day and will not be quiet until they happen.

I have read Jeremiah. I have listened to Isaiah. Words from Hosea and Zechariah and Ezekiel pulsate within me. I cannot rest, will not rest, do not want to rest until I see with my own eyes what the Lord has spoken!

That is the reason why I and others, Jew and Gentile together, traveled to Spain to pray in the room where Ferdinand and Isabella signed the decree to evict the Jews from Spain and confiscate their wealth. We wanted to confess the sins of our people and to ask the Lord to cover our sins with His blood. We wanted to pray that the Lord would restore us to each other.

That is why we sat in the dust together in shame and grief after seeing the chains on the wall of the San Juan de los Reyes cathedral in Toledo, Spain.

That is why we Gentiles formed a reception line for our Jewish brothers and sisters when we visited the ruins of Nicea. These brothers had not been invited to the earlier councils, and we were grieving their loss and exclusion.

That is why some of us who are non-Jews went to the annual meetings of the Messianic Jewish Alliance of America and the Union of Messianic Jewish Congregations and knelt before the entire assembly to confess our own sins and the sins of generations preceding us. We love our Jewish family and we want to be with them!

Have mercy on us, Lord! Change our hearts! O Lord, listen! O Lord, forgive! O Lord, hear and act! For Your sake, O my God, do not delay!

Lord, raise up Daniels, Ezras and Nehemiahs in our day, men who will see what You have intended and who will stay before You until the vision is accomplished. Raise up the Ruths and Rahabs who will experience Your presence, who will covenant with You and with Your people to usher in Your work.

With the psalmist we say, "If I forget you, O Jerusalem, may my right hand forget its skill. May my tongue cling to the roof of my mouth if I do not remember you, if I do not consider Jerusalem my highest joy" (137:5–6).

Through their Israel Prayer Mission, Leonardo and Una Bella spend their time mobilizing and equipping an ever-expanding prayer army of over four thousand committed saints from the nations, praying to tear down enemy strongholds that stand between Israel and her Messiah Yeshua. They meet people daily who have never had a valid witness of Jesus in their lives. They invite them into their home to share the good news and to live life together. Their passion is to see each Israeli "pre-believer" exposed to the living reality of the kingdom of heaven in the here and now, believing that each must be nurtured and prepared for the revelation of Yeshua that can only come through the Holy Spirit in God's perfect timing.

Remarks from Leonardo and Una Bella,
Israel Prayer Mission

Leonardo: Una, my wife, grew up in Israel and I in New York. It is a stark fact that no one had ever shared the good news with us to the point where we could even reject it. Our families were secular, and as adults, Una and I were very New Age in our beliefs and understanding. Coming from Israel, Una had a deep allergic reaction to anything to do with Yeshua. Above all, the concept of our being sinners or needing any form of atonement for sin was completely foreign to us. In the year 2000 we were living in Maui, Hawaii, and if you'd asked us the day before we came to faith if we would ever become born-again believers in Yeshua, we would have emphatically stated, "Never!" The grace-filled miracle of our salvation came in response to the fervent prayers of Una's cousin and his family twelve thousand miles away in Israel! Her cousin is a pioneering believer in the Land, and he and his wife and children had been praying for us faithfully for a year without our knowledge.

Nine months into being prayed for, I came upon a tattered King James Bible in the bottom of a box in someone's garage and asked if I could take it. This alone was strange, since we had only mocked the Bible. The next morning I awoke with a start, tumbled downstairs and opened to Matthew's gospel and started reading. Because of the Old English wording, I would often have to repeat a phrase over and over before I grasped it. I read for hours and finally announced to Una that I was born again, and wanted to be baptized.

Una: I was horrified, but I didn't say anything at the time. I simply went into the next room and muttered, "God, not that I believe in You, but if You do exist, why do You insist on ruining my marriage and my life?" Over the next days, my strategy was not to argue with my husband, hoping that his new passion would soon fade away.

Born and raised in Israel, I was taught all my life that Yeshua was the reason my mom's aunts and uncles were killed in the Holocaust. The New Testament was a forbidden book—even to touch. But as my husband was reading it, a thought popped into my mind that had never occurred to me before: *I wonder who Yeshua is.*

The next morning as I looked into the mirror, Yeshua was looking back at me. He revealed Himself in His suffering with a crown of thorns and a bloodied face—the only way I had ever pictured Him. He looked at me with more love than I ever knew existed. I had so many deep questions, and for the next six months, He came to me over and over and lovingly brought me revelations and explanations directly. It is a fact that my cousin's prayers were answered that moment I said with a true heart, "I wonder who Yeshua really is."

God reached out and grabbed our hearts straight from heaven as the result of prayer. We believe that the loving and steadfast prayers of true believers will bring about healing and open the minds and hearts of our people Israel.

13

The Final Exodus

> They overcame him by the blood of the Lamb and by the
> word of their testimony; they did not love their lives so much
> as to shrink from death.
>
> Revelation 12:11

For almost four hundred years, Israel had languished in Goshen.
Father Jacob's assurance that they would be rescued from this
foreign land was a vague dream. Then one day things began to
happen. There were rumblings that an exit was imminent—reports
of miracles. These reports were often confusing, since Pharaoh's
magicians were also producing "signs." Then other marvels—a
series of plagues that not even the court sorcerers could mimic.
The faithful God-followers in the area of Goshen were marvel-
ously protected from the plagues but faced the fury of the incensed
taskmasters of Egypt.

The last plague was released on Passover night. The blood of
a slain lamb, painted on the doorposts, was the sign of obedience necessary to protect Israel's firstborn sons. Death reigned in

Egypt that night, from the house of Pharaoh even to the livestock in the fields. Wails of grief could be heard throughout the land. In Goshen, the Israelites were quietly sequestered behind blood-stained doors. Not even a dog barked to disturb the peace (see Exodus 11:7).

The yearned-for moment had arrived. At midnight the call went forth. Israel was released from her centuries-old slavery. God was calling her home.

One final hurdle lay ahead—the crossing of the Red Sea. According to every visible assessment, defeat seemed sure. Hemmed in by the approaching chariots of Pharaoh in swift pursuit behind them and the deep waters in front of them, there was no escape. But the Lord fought for Israel that night. The waters of the sea divided and a pillar of fire lighted the exit route for the two million Israelites leaving Egypt.

Today we stand poised for another great exodus. It has not been four hundred but two thousand years since Yeshua said to His disciples, "I will come back and take you to be with me" (John 14:3).

For two millennia the family of Messiah has languished in a foreign country, waiting for His return. Today there are rumblings that another exodus is imminent. The signposts to which He pointed—the events that would take place before His return—are appearing.

Three significant, predicted signs indicate that the day is near: (1) Israel's second exodus from the nations to the land of her inheritance is in progress; (2) Jewish people are recognizing their Messiah; (3) the world is in its all-time grand revival of faith in the one true God and His promised Messiah.

The day when the skies will part to welcome His return is fast approaching. Luke and Zechariah agree that He will return to the Mount of Olives (see Zechariah 14:4; Acts 1:11). John and Isaiah describe an earthly reign of peace (see Isaiah 65:18–25; Revelation 20:1–6). In His first advent, Jesus was the Suffering Servant. This time He will come as conquering King.

Modern-Day Plagues

In spite of growing anticipation of our exodus and the Lord's return, there are difficult days ahead. Jesus spoke not only of uneasy times surrounding Jerusalem's destruction, but also of global labor pangs preceding His arrival.

We can expect a proliferation of miracle-working messiahs and prophets (see Mark 13:22). Wars and rivalry between nations (*ethnos*, "ethnic groups") will increase (see Matthew 24:6–7). Famines and earthquakes will multiply. Wickedness will mature alongside world revival and apostasy (verses 12–14). "Distress, unequaled from the beginning of the world until now—and never to be equaled again" (verse 21) will descend upon a Church waiting to be delivered. If it were possible (which, thanks be to God, it is not for those who look to Him), even the people of God would be deceived (verse 24).

Paul speaks of the anti-messiah, the end-time Pharaoh, the personification of evil—Satan's own personal representative—who will unite the world against God's people for one last battle before the exodus (see 2 Thessalonians 2:8–12). Daniel saw that the saints will be "handed over to him for a time" (see Daniel 7:25) and that only those faithful to God will be able to resist him (see 11:32). Zechariah speaks of a time when the whole world will come with Pharaoh-force against Israel (and those who are covenanted with her); in that moment the Lord will ensure her safety (see Zechariah 12:3; 14:2–3).

"But, wait!" you may be saying. "I thought we would be gone before then! Is not the Church to be raptured before this last great tribulation?"

Some believe we will. Others point to the scriptural indications that we must endure the coming "plagues" before our departure.

An interesting Greek word, *thlipsis,* often translated "tribulation" in our English Bibles, gives weight to this understanding. The word can also be translated "anguish, affliction, sufferings, persecution, trouble, hardship, distress, oppression," or even "pressure and stress." Fifty times this word is used in the apostolic writings, often to warn believers that they are not exempt from difficult times.

"Be careful that you do not fall away because of trouble (*thlipsis*) or persecution," Jesus warned (Matthew 13:21, author's paraphrase). In fact, "In this world you will have trouble (*thlipsis*). But take heart! I have overcome the world" (John 16:33).

Paul picked up the theme of enduring many hardships (*thlipsis*) to enter the kingdom (see Acts 14:22), and encouraging believers to be "patient in affliction (*thlipsis*)" (Romans 12:12). Believe it or not, we are to "rejoice in our sufferings (*thlipsis*)" (5:3).

When Jesus was speaking of the end times, He told the apostles that the sign of the Son of Man will appear, the *shofar* (trumpet) will sound and the Lord will gather His elect "immediately after the distress (*thlipsis*) of those days" (Matthew 24:29). John, in his vision, saw a great multitude from every nation, tribe, people and language standing before the throne. "These are they *who have come out of the great tribulation (thlipsis)*," one of the elders told John (Revelation 7:14, emphasis mine). One has to have been *in* the Great Tribulation before he or she can come *out* of it.

I could be wrong, but I would rather be prepared for the worst and be delivered than to be caught off guard. Come to think of it, if the Lord will allow me sufficient strength, I would like to be here to serve during those perilous times.

Are You Ready to Suffer?

We in the West have experienced little serious persecution for our faith in recent years. That is not the case in much of the world. Daily there are reports of cruelty and martyrdom. In India a seasoned missionary and his two sons were trapped in their car and burned to death by Hindu extremists protesting the proclamation of the Gospel of Jesus.

The Christian population in the Sudan has been almost annihilated by rebel forces determined to eradicate the Christian faith.[1]
Uganda is still recovering from the death toll exacted during Idi
Amin's reign of terror.[2] In Iraq and other Muslim nations, new believers are often put to death by their own family members to "protect"
the family honor. Coptic Christians were beheaded before a watching
world by radical Islamic terrorists. At the same time, there are tens
of thousands of new believers because of the faithfulness of those
who have risked their lives to spread the good news of the Savior.

As the time of Messiah's return draws near, the warfare will
only escalate. Evil and righteousness are maturing together until
the harvest, just as Jesus told His listeners in explaining one of
the parables (see Matthew 13:30). John sees that harvest in a vision: angels released to gather the righteous into their reward;
the wicked thrown into the winepress of the Lord's wrath (see
Revelation 14:14–20).

Believers may go through great tribulation, but they will never
experience God's wrath. We have been saved from the "coming
wrath" through the blood of the Messiah that has been applied,
by faith, to the doorposts of our hearts (see Romans 5:9; 1 Thessalonians 5:9).

In times of great persecution, many die for their faith. For others, the Lord stays the hand of torturers and executioners.

While in prayer, a sister imprisoned in China felt the shackles
drop from her wrists—not unlike Peter's prison experience. Two
men on bicycles escaped the secret police, who were pursuing them
in a patrol car—the cyclists could be seen but not caught—reminiscent of Pharaoh's thwarted pursuit of Israel at the sea.[3] During
the days of Communism, a brother in Ethiopia was beaten mer-
cilessly for preaching the Gospel and walked away the following
day completely healed—like Paul in an earlier century. Twice that
same brother was scheduled for execution by electrocution. Both
times a mysterious power failure kept him alive. The frustrated
executioners finally released him.[4]

Visible angel warriors and other heavenly messengers are not uncommon in days of great stress. God is carefully watching over His flock to deliver some *from* persecution, while others are being given strength *in* persecution.

The assaults against believers come through human hands, but the plans all have their origin in hell. The Holy Spirit wants us to learn to trust the Lord to care for us, just as He watched over Israel in Goshen, over Daniel in the lions' den, over the early apostles in years of imprisonment, exile or even death. He wants us to have the tenacity of Daniel's friends, who said before being thrown into the blazing furnace, "The God we serve is able to save us. . . . But even if he does not, we want you to know, O king, that we will not serve your gods" (Daniel 3:17–18).

Yes, sometime in the future the whole world will take a stand against Israel. All the nations will gather against Jerusalem and bow to a godless ruler. When that day comes, we believers must be ready to come alongside God's covenant people. At that point, our earthly nationality—whether American, Asian, African, Middle Eastern or another—will no longer be important. All that will matter is that we are born-again-into-the-kingdom fellow citizens with Israel.

Sometime in the future the whole world will take a stand against Israel. Then our earthly nationality will no longer be important. All that will matter is that we are born-again-into-the-kingdom fellow citizens with Israel.

During the closing days of our stay in "Egypt," our focus is steady. We must rescue others, we must stay in the house with the Lamb's blood on the door and we must be ready to go at a moment's notice. We want to be sure our spiritual cloaks are tucked into our belts, our sandals are on our feet, our staff is in hand and we are ready to depart (see Exodus 12:11). When the call comes, the exodus will be abrupt. "In its time I will do this swiftly," Isaiah quotes the Lord (60:22). "In a flash, in the twinkling of an eye," Paul comments (1 Corinthians 15:52).

Centuries of anticipation will give way to a single "suddenly" (Malachi 3:1). Clouds will part, the earth will shake and angel choirs and the redeemed of Adam's children will welcome the returning Messiah. His reign of peace will extend for a thousand years, according to John, before the war to end all wars and the final defeat of mankind's archenemy (see Revelation 20:7–11).

Only then will the Garden of Eden be restored and heaven and earth joined as God and man—Redeemer and redeemed—dwell together in eternal bliss.

Remarks from Dan Juster,
Tikkun Ministries International, Jerusalem, Israel

One noted Bible scholar taught me that while there is one interpretive meaning to the Word in Scripture, there are yet multiple times of fulfillment. Each time of fulfillment is more intense, more extensive and more powerful than the time before. Iain Murray, in his book *The Puritan Hope*, asserted that the Puritans understood the progression of history as a series of revivals. As each revival ebbs, another will come. Finally, there will be a grand world revival that will lead to the Second Coming of Yeshua.

So this is the nature of history—times of progress and times when evil seems to work its will on earth. We look at the exodus from Egypt as foreshadowing of the events of the very end of this age. The Olivet Discourses point to the upheaval of the first century, but also to the final upheaval before the return of the Lord (see Matthew 24, Mark 13, Luke 21). It is difficult to tell when to apply the text to the first century and when to apply it to the final end.

However, we can clearly see the progression and the parallels. After the exodus came the revelation of the glory of God on Sinai and then the glory of God filling the tabernacle at the end of the book of Exodus. The upheavals of the first century and the pain of the tribulation of those days was also accompanied by a great harvest, beginning with the Jewish harvest at *Shavuot* (Pentecost). This led to a harvest from the nations, but also to the painful destruction of the second Temple and the destruction of Jerusalem.

The End of Days, the last of the last days, however, is again a time of plagues, upheaval, tribulation and again a time of great harvest. There is a harvest of the Jewish people (see Revelation 7 and the 144,000 from all the tribes of Israel) and a harvest from every nation, tongue and people. Darkness and light will be in great contrast, but the eternal Gospel will go forth (see Revelation 14:6–7). Then He will come to rule and reign forever, and we who have embraced this eternal Gospel will rule with Him.

So let us be ready for the last great Passover and Exodus!

Blessed to Be a Blessing

> I will bless those who bless you, and whoever curses you I
> will curse.
>
> Genesis 12:3

While visiting in Ethiopia in April 1999, we became well-acquainted
with a man who had served in the royal house of Haile Selassie
I, the last emperor of Ethiopia. Haile Selassie, believed by many
to have been the 225th descendant of Menelik, the son of King
Solomon and the Queen of Sheba, was emperor of Ethiopia from
1930 until 1974. Here is what he told us.

In the early '70s, under pressure from some of the surrounding Arab nations, Selassie broke diplomatic relations with Israel.
When his daughter heard the news, she went to her father to warn
him of the consequences of his actions. Referring to the Genesis
12:3 blessing on the house of Abraham, she implored him, "My
father, my king, you will bring disaster upon our family and upon
our people!"

Not many months later, on September 12, 1974, Lieutenant Colonel Mengistu Haile Miriam, one of Africa's fiercest dictators, seized the reins of power in Ethiopia. Soon afterward Haile Selassie was dead, killed by the man who had engineered his downfall. This event was followed by almost two decades of bloodshed.

Haile Selassie's daughter was right. Whoever touches Israel touches the "apple of [God's] eye" (Zechariah 2:8).

Egypt discovered that truth very early in Israel's history. Assyria and Babylon, after being used of God to punish Israel for her disobedience, nevertheless sank into oblivion as world powers soon after their years of cruel tyranny. Spain's navy ruled the seas—until that country killed or expelled her Jewish population. There was a time when the sun never set on the British Empire; that was before Great Britain reneged on the Balfour Declaration. Germany was split in two following the Holocaust, but a growing number of believers in Germany have taken upon themselves the sins of their forefathers and are now godly intercessors and advocates for Israel and the Jewish people. The Communist governments of Eastern Europe crumbled after years of pogroms and persecution against God's favored son.

The United States has walked in enormous blessing and prosperity through the years as millions of Jewish people have found refuge on our shores, but recent governmental decisions against Israel, our most loyal ally in the Middle East, are rapidly bringing that blessing to a close. Judgment has already fallen on our land following the pressure to evacuate parts of Israel and divide up their land (see Joel 3:1–2).

Zechariah speaks of a time when all the nations of the world will wage war against this one small country (see 14:2). United Nations' resolutions in recent years have come dangerously close to Zechariah's prediction.

"What has all this to do with me?" you may ask. "I was not a Crusader who burned Jewish synagogues. None of my relatives (as far as I know) were Nazis who sent Jews to the gas chambers. I don't hate Jews."

Though we may not be personally responsible for the indignities suffered by our Jewish brothers and sisters through the years, there are steps we can take to reverse the injustices and actively bless the Jewish people.

Ask the Lord to cleanse our hearts of every vestige of anti-Semitism.

This includes ethnic jokes, gossip and insinuation. A "funny" story or cynical remark will only encourage more discrimination against this persecuted family.

Hatred for the Jews may be buried deeply in our souls, amid the debris of generations of prejudice. We may not even be aware of its presence until we find ourselves joining in the derision.

If God is not finished with Israel, if Israel is destined to accept her Messiah and usher in a future reign of Jesus, if the Church is an heir together with Israel rather than an heir in place of Israel and if we have believed to the contrary, then we must repent of having appropriated Jewish Scriptures and Israel's promises for our own without having honored the very people to whom they were originally granted and without including them as part of the Bride of Messiah.

Let the winds of the Holy Spirit blow your heart clean. Reach back in time and listen to God's heart for this priestly nation. Understand why world hatred has been launched against them, and allow God's love to rise up to bless them.

Once our own hearts are clean, we can become intercessors— those who stand in the gap. Like Daniel, we can agonize in prayer, taking upon ourselves the sins of past generations, asking for mercy: "Our sins and the iniquities of our fathers have made Jerusalem and your people an object of scorn. . . . O Lord, listen! O Lord, forgive! O Lord, hear and act! For your sake, O my God, do not delay, because your city and your people bear your Name" (Daniel 9:16, 19).

Become aware that the world's news media is prejudiced against God's work and God's people.

Only those who are God-followers can properly assess history, politics and government. Everything in human history, every current event, is moving forward in His timing. We, therefore, will listen to news with greater discernment, always asking ourselves such questions as, "What is the real story behind this report? What is the Lord doing? How am I to be praying here? How am I to respond?"

Seek ways to affirm Jewish people, to love them and bless them— whether or not they ever accept Jesus as Messiah.

Jesus spoke of two commandments upon which hang all the Law and the Prophets—loving God and loving each other (see Matthew 22:34–40). Love is active, not passive. We do not love those we ignore, as Jesus so convincingly taught us in the parable of the Good Samaritan.

Just because we have not participated in the Crusades or pogroms of past years does not excuse our passive disinterest in the recurring rise of anti-Semitism throughout the world. If we are not actively righteous, we become passively wicked.

Is there a Jewish community in your neighborhood? Do they have gatherings to which non-Jews are invited? Become informed. Get acquainted with your Jewish neighbors. Become their friends. You may even feel the need to apologize for never having taken a stand for the Jewish people. According to the Prophets, a time will yet come when they will need our friendship.

Over and over again, even in our own nation, assaults have been made against the Jewish people. Not that long ago, a friend of mine was in Sacramento when three of the city's five synagogues were desecrated in one night of cowardly tyranny. Millions of dollars' worth of damage was left behind by demonized arsonists. My friend suggested that Christians unite to rebuild the vandalized synagogues. "Oh, and let's save the tracts and the evangelism for another time," he said. "This is a time for blessing with actions."

Paul spoke of living in such a way that makes His people jealous (see Romans 11:11). That will never happen if all we do is hand out tracts and get into arguments and debates.

Our commitment to Jewish people must never be tied to their acceptance of Yeshua as Messiah. We have been down that road before, and it has produced no fruit. If there were never to be another Jewish person in history who believes in Jesus as Messiah, we must still be committed to them as friends, brothers, protectors. Any other action is incongruous with a heart of love.

> *If there were never to be another Jewish person in history who believes in Jesus as Messiah, we must still be committed to them as friends, brothers, protectors.*

Prepare for future crises.

On Christmas morning 1999, a group of famous Israelis were being interviewed on national television in Israel about their impressions of Yeshua. Professor Ravitsky, a well-known orthodox scholar, said he realized that had Yeshua been alive in Germany during World War II, He would have been taken to the gas chambers.[1]

Would you have risked your life to save His? Would I? What will I do the next time? These are the kinds of questions we Christians must ask ourselves as we prepare for the future.

Some of my friends are actually building shelters—secret hideaways—to house Jewish people in the coming persecution. Christians in Finland and the rest of Scandinavia have stored food and clothing, bought vehicles for transportation and made other preparations for the next great exodus of Israel's children coming from Russia and the Eastern bloc nations. They want to be the Oskar Schindlers and the Corrie ten Booms, the "righteous Gentiles"—as the Jewish people call them—of our generation.

Encourage and assist Jewish people to return to their ancestral inheritance.

If Ezekiel's word about "not leaving any behind" (Ezekiel 39:28) is to be taken literally—and remember, this is our assumption unless Scripture clearly indicates otherwise—then we also need to do our best to make sure they make *aliyah* to Israel.

In 1973, Steve Lightle gave up his business and began to travel throughout Europe and Russia, speaking prophetically about the imminent release of the Russian Jewish population. In 1983 he wrote *Exodus II* to encourage continued readiness.[2] Tom Hess established the Jerusalem House of Prayer for All Nations and then published his book *Let My People Go* to describe a partnership with God in the prophetic fulfillment that was beginning to take place.[3]

Hess writes,

Many Jewish people have believed that Israel's security is in the military and financial support coming from America. The Jewish people need to be warned that while the support of America has in many ways been a blessing in the past, the future support of Israel will increasingly come from God Himself and, hopefully, from her loyal Christian Zionist friends around the world.[4]

It is time for the Jewish people in America to set an example for the Russian Jews. It is time to break from the god of materialism in America and to take whatever wealth they have in America back to Israel as they did from Egypt and Babylon centuries ago! . . . It is time for the Jews to escape the Daughter of Babylon before it is too late.[5]

Precious Jewish people, make Aliyah very soon. Don't wait until you have to go. Win the struggle and escape to Israel today. Come singing and dancing with joy and gladness in Zion, preparing the way for the soon coming of your Messiah and King![6]

Gustav Scheller devoted the last years of his life to an organization aiding tens of thousands of Jewish people from Eastern Europe to immigrate to Israel. That story is told in *Operation Exodus*.[7] David and Emma Rudolph have established Gateways Beyond to help not only the Eastern Europeans, but also Ethiopian Jews, many of whom are trapped between the two lands. Ethiopians discriminate against them because they are Jews; Israel will not accept many of them because they do not have the proper papers to prove their identity.

Bless the Jewish people financially . . .

We have already seen how Paul, the Jewish apostle to the Gentiles, incorporated the Jew-Gentile issue into his Roman letter. In the closing verses of this epistle, he makes it clear that "if the Gentiles have shared in the Jews' spiritual blessings, *they owe it to the Jews to share with them their material blessings*" (Romans 15:27, emphasis added).

Of course, we know Isaiah predicted that "the wealth on the seas will be brought" (Isaiah 60:5), that their gates will remain open "so that men may bring you the wealth of the nations" (verse 11). Millions of dollars have poured into the reestablishing of the nation since that first Zionist conference in 1897.

A fascinating—even miraculous—story of the days preceding the 1948 War of Independence involves Golda Meir, the late prime minister of Israel from 1969 to 1974. Morale in Israel was at its lowest ebb. There was no money for tanks, artillery or aircraft for the war that was sure to come the moment Israel announced its statehood in May of that year. Golda Meir insisted that David ben Gurion should remain at the helm while she, Golda, traveled to the United States to gather funds. There was little hope for the success of this unpretentious, straight-talking carpenter's daughter.

Golda left Israel with no baggage, wearing only a thin spring dress and clutching her almost-empty handbag. She landed in New

York City with ten dollars in her purse and no scheduled speaking appointments. When she returned to Israel only a few days later, the American Jewish community had committed fifty million dollars with which to equip the small Israeli army.[8]

Since that time, the Gentile community, too—especially Christians who have been reading prophecy—have come to Israel's aid. After Israel took Jerusalem in the Six-Day War of 1967, the United States and other nations refused to move their embassies to the new capital. The International Christian Embassy Jerusalem (ICEJ) was formed to assure Israel that thousands of Christians throughout the world disagreed with the decision of their governments. Millions of dollars of support have been funneled to Israel through the efforts of this and similar organizations.

. . . especially the family of believers.

As we grow in understanding, we will also be sure that in our "doing good," we give "especially to those who belong to the family of believers" (Galatians 6:10). Large sums of money are sometimes given by zealous Israel-loving Christians to Jewish organizations that persecute the Messianic believers in the Land. Paul's emphasis was always on believers, and he was especially careful to remember the poor (see Rom. 15:26; Gal. 2:10).

As more and more Christians understand Paul's admonition—that we owe it to the Jewish people to bless them financially—we can expect individual Christians and churches and denominational and independent mission agencies to prioritize the financial needs of Israel and the Jewish people, especially the Messianic community.

A Messianic congregation north of Haifa, whose synagogue was firebombed by those who did not like their message, was later able to purchase a ministry center three times the size of the one that was burned. The arsonists were used of God to alert Christians to the need for a larger and more secure facility! More resources flowed into the same synagogue later, following the vandalism in which tires were slashed while a worship service was in session. More and more Messianic congregations and ministries have been able to purchase their own buildings and are now a more recognized part of the Israeli Jewish community.

Become wise in the distribution of funds.

It is imperative that we become wise in the distribution of funds. Ask the Lord to open your eyes. Watch where the fruit is being produced rather than becoming carried away by someone who is a great communicator but who may have little fruit to show for years of fund-raising. Attaching the names Israel and Jerusalem to a letterhead can sometimes, perhaps unintentionally, produce sympathy for a ministry that may have a big name but little to show for it, and that has little connection with the real laborers in the field. Get to know the restored remnant, the actual Jewish believers living in the Land, who are giving themselves to the miraculous latter-day restoration of Messianic faith where it all began. Become informed. Support those who have effective ministries.

Establish prayer support groups to share in the ministry of those who are on the front lines of the battles.

In Nashville, as in many cities of the world, prayer for Israel and the Jewish people runs deep in the veins of many intercessors and ministries that are linked to several key ministries, both in the Land and in the Diaspora. We welcome Messianic Jewish leaders to the city and become prayer partners with them. Their needs become our needs; their joys, our joys; their sorrows, our sorrows. We are often in daily contact through email and can participate with them more effectively, bearing one another's burdens (see Galatians 6:2). We are workers together with God as Paul told the Ephesians (see 2:10), participating in what He initiates. Plans are laid to establish our own prayer center that will connect to those in major cities of the world who are in agreement with the prophetic call upon our Jewish brothers and sisters.

I have been to Israel several times. The first time—in 1967, shortly before the Six-Day War—I had no knowledge of prophecy or of God's purposes for Israel. I only wanted to walk where Jesus walked.

Today when I visit, I go for the purpose of blessing the people of the Land. I encourage every traveler to tithe the cost of the ticket to one of the ministries inside Israel and to look for opportunities to serve, to bless, to give.

I further encourage all my brothers and sisters not to leave the Land before becoming acquainted with some of those who are investing their lives in seeing that their own people come to know Israel's Messiah. I am eager for other Christians to see the passion blazing in Asher Intrater's eyes when he speaks of the Lord. To behold the joy on Eitan Shishkoff's face when he welcomes new believers into the family. To watch the love flowing through Leon Matzin, Israel Pochtar or others as they wrap their arms around former Russian youth and others who have now met the Man. To worship in Avner and Rachel Boskey's living room as this anointed couple brings forth their prophetic Hebrew songs.

The Lord may give you other ways to bless and to love Jewish people. Jesus told Nicodemus that being born again is by the wind/breath of the Spirit (see John 3:8). We lift our sails to discern the wind and feel the breath of God.

Today the Spirit is blowing Israel back to her Land and breathing new life into Jewish hearts as they open to the good news of their Messiah, who has come and will soon return. At the same time, He is sweeping like a tempest across the nations, stirring up the grandest revival of faith in the one true God and His Redeemer-Son that Abraham's children have ever known.

If you are a believer, that same Holy Spirit lives in your heart. Listen to Him and follow where He leads.

Today a new thing is happening among many Christians throughout the world. We see ourselves as Ruth—the non-Jew who has come to faith in Israel's Redeemer. We have come from the famine. We have found bread in the house of our Kinsman-Redeemer, Boaz (Jesus).

We are now beginning to go through the house to look for Moabite ways that need to be eliminated in order to restore the furnishings of Israel. We are committing ourselves anew not only to Jesus, Boaz and Ruth's promised Son, but to His relatives. We are welcoming again the customs of the family into which we have been adopted.

We have watched in the past as this family of ours has been persecuted and maligned. We grieve with our brothers and sisters over their pain, which was often inflicted at the hands of our own ancestors in the faith.

We are saying to our Jewish family: "Your people shall be my people, and your God, my God" (Ruth 1:16 NKJV). A growing number of us are stirred in our spirits. We are ready to make a bold declaration—one that might be tested at any moment. We are ready to say with Ruth (see verse 17): I am ready to die with you and be buried with you. May the Lord deal with me, be it ever so severely, if anything but death separates you and me.

Afterword

"So just what exactly is Don Finto doing now?"

In the twenty years since Don stepped aside as senior pastor of Belmont Church in 1996 and started the Caleb Company, as well as the fifteen years since *Your People* was first published, I have heard that question—in one form or another—more times than I could begin to count. As anyone who knows Don can attest, there is no simple response: in part because of Don's energy and commitment to pursuing the things of the Lord, and in part because of the doors that have continued to open to him in that pursuit. At the same time, three anecdotes help illustrate that journey, its impact on so many of us and the passion behind the book you have just read.

The first occurred about a year ago when my wife and I were having dinner with a well-known pastor and his family, longtime lovers of Israel. Halfway through the evening, this pastor turned to me and, out of the blue, asked, "How are things going with Don Finto in his call to enlighten the Church that God has not turned His back on the Jewish people?" I remember pausing before responding, not because I didn't know how Don was or what he

197

was doing at the time, but because I appreciated that the question represented a fair start to one of the foundational aspects of insight Don has received—and shared—over the last twenty years.

The foundational aspect? That the principles of Romans 11 continue in full certainty: (a) God has not cast away His chosen people; (b) Israel's rejection of her own Messiah is temporary; (c) that rejection has opened up the opportunity of salvation for Gentiles; (d) we, as Gentiles, are to be humbly supportive of the return and re-grafting of the "original branches" of God's olive tree, for (e) when those branches begin to return, unprecedented benefit results. And the cornerstone truth: The gifts and calling of God on the Jewish people are irrevocable.

The second incident, several years ago, took place in a local bakery where Don has been known to exercise his appreciation for cinnamon buns. As he was leaving, he passed a table of three ladies, two of whom were believers with whom he was acquainted and the third a non-believing member of the Jewish community. As they spoke, the Jewish lady asked, "Are you trying to convert all the Jews?" In a characteristically kind response, he replied, "Oh, no! We just want you to know your own Messiah!"

The point to be made is reasonably self-evident: Commitment to the God of Abraham, Isaac and Jacob inherently includes a deep commitment to His chosen people and an abiding heart for their salvation.

The third encounter was a few years ago in Pennsylvania, where families of Messianic Jews had gathered from the United States and Israel for a weekend conference; Don and I were the only Gentiles present. One afternoon session involved men only, and began with an extended worship session, complete with traditional dancing. Time seemed to hold its breath as first-generation believers and their grown and teenage sons sang and danced together for almost two hours in vibrant worship to the point of physical exhaustion. And, of course, then-75-year-old Don was in the middle of it all! In that setting, I saw him manifest as the father in the faith that virtually none of those re-grafted men and their believing sons had experienced in their pursuit of Yeshua as Messiah. And just as he has done with generations of Gentiles, Don spent the rest of the afternoon and evening encouraging individuals and groups of those Jewish men in their walk with the Lord.

That afternoon, the "one new man" of Ephesians 2 became a practical and physical reality as Jew and Gentile became one in honoring the Lord. Of equal significance the promises of 2,600 years ago, found in Ezekiel 37, began to be fulfilled: that the "dry bones" of the "whole house of Israel" would experience rebirth as the literal breath of God (the Holy Spirit) begins to move over His people, giving them "life from the dead."

There is much more, of course. The revelation that Don began to experience in 1996 continues to unfold, grow and take on greater importance, even as belief among Jewish people in Yeshua as Messiah reaches levels not seen since the first century CE. Even now, at a remarkably young 86, Don sees his calling as a latter-day Caleb, positioned to take the mountain of his inheritance as yet another generation joins him in ministering the Gospel of the kingdom to Jew and Gentile alike.

My prayerful hope is that *Your People Shall Be My People* will serve as a catalyst for you to consider joining Don and Caleb Company in this unparalleled work. And may the promised blessing of Genesis 12:3 be yours as you do. *Shalom* in Yeshua.

David Hooper, attorney, founding chairman of the board,
Caleb Company

Appendix A

Toward Jerusalem Council II

Toward Jerusalem Council II is an initiative of repentance and reconciliation between the Jewish and Gentile segments of the Church. The vision is that one day there will be a second Council of Jerusalem that will be, in an important aspect, the inverse of the first council described in Acts 15. Whereas the first council was made up of Jewish believers in Yeshua (Jesus), who decided not to impose on the Gentiles the requirements of the Jewish Law, so the second council would be made up of Gentile Church leaders, who would recognize and welcome the Jewish believers in Yeshua without requiring them to abandon their Jewish identity and practice.

The initiative is led by an executive committee, both Jewish and Gentile members representative of the different international movements and churches, historic and modern, that confess Yeshua (Jesus) as Lord and Savior. The committee members offer themselves as servants of this vision:

To make known to Church leaders and Christian scholars the restoration of the Jewish segments of the Church (the Church of the circumcision).

To foster repentance for the sins of the Gentile Christians and the Christian Church against the Jewish people, especially for the suppression of the corporate Jewish witness to Yeshua, the Messiah.

To foster intercession for all the Churches of the nations to abandon all forms of replacement teaching concerning the calling and election of Israel and to recognize the place of the Jew in the body of Messiah.

To encourage the messianic Jewish community in and out of Israel to enter into this vision of reconciliation and restoration and thereby foster unity among the different streams and organizations within the messianic Jewish movement.

The executive committee will seek to do everything possible to forward a convocation of a second Council of Jerusalem. This can only happen under the special leading of the Holy Spirit. Only the Holy Spirit can show us how a council recognized by all churches, denominations and movements can be possible.

Within this process toward a second Council of Jerusalem there would be a gathering in Jerusalem, with as many representatives of churches/denominations and contingents as possible, for the purpose of issuing a call to the whole Christian world for the recognition of the Church of the circumcision at a second Council of Jerusalem.

We are doing this so that God may be honored in the reconciling work of His Son through the healing of the original schism in the Body of Christ between the Jewish and the Gentile components.

The ultimate purpose in unifying the Body and restoring the Jewish believers to their rightful place is the hastening of the coming of the Lord Yeshua in glory and the full accomplishment of His work in the kingdom of God.

> If their rejection [means] the reconciliation of the world, what will their acceptance [mean] but life from the dead?
>
> Romans 11:15

For more information, you may contact the TJCII executive general secretary at www.tjcii.org.

Appendix B

Recommended Reading

Bennett, Ramon. *When Day and Night Cease: A Prophetic Study of World Events and How Prophecy Concerning Israel Affects the Nations, the Church and You*. Jerusalem: Arm of Salvation Press, 1992.

Brown, Michael L. *Our Hands Are Stained with Blood: The Tragic Story of the "Church" and the Jewish People*. Shippensburg, Penn.: Destiny Image Publishers, 1992.

Cantor, Ron. *I Am Not Ashamed*. Gaithersburg, Md.: Tikkun International, 1999.

_____ *Identity Theft*. Shippensburg, Penn.: Destiny Image, 2013.

Chernoff, Yohanna. *Born a Jew . . . Die a Jew: The Story of Martin Chernoff, a Pioneer in Messianic Judaism*. Hagerstown, Md.: EBED Publications, 1996.

Collins, Larry and Dominique Lapierre. *O Jerusalem! Day by Day and Minute by Minute: The Historic Struggle for Jerusalem and the Birth of Israel*. New York: Simon and Schuster, 1972.

Damkani, Jacob. *Why Me?* New Kensington, Penn.: Whitaker House, 1997.

205

Dolan, David. *Israel at the Crossroads, Fifty Years and Counting.* Grand Rapids, Mich.: Fleming H. Revell, 1998.

Doron, Reuven. *One New Man.* Cedar Rapids, Iowa: Embrace Israel, 1996.

Finto, Don. *God's Promise and the Future of Israel: Compelling Questions People Ask About Israel and the Middle East.* Bloomington, Minn.: Chosen Books, 2006.

_____*PREPARE! for the End Time Harvest.* Nashville, Tenn.: Caleb Publications, 2015.

Flynn, Leslie B. *What the Church Owes the Jew.* Carlsbad, Calif.: Magnus Press, 1998.

Frydland, Rachmiel. *What the Rabbis Know About the Messiah, A Study of Genealogy and Prophecy.* Cincinnati, Ohio: Messianic Publishing Company, 1991.

Goldberg-Distefano, Gari. *An Unexpected Miracle.* Mustang, Okla.: Tate Publishing, 2014.

Goll, James W. *The Coming Israel Awakening: Gazing into the Future of the Jewish People and the Church.* Grand Rapids, Mich., Chosen Books, 2001, 2009.

Heidler, Robert D. *The Messianic Church Arising!* Denton, Tex.: Glory of Zion International Ministries, 2006.

Hess, Tom. *Let My People Go: The Struggle of the Jewish People to Return to Israel,* 5th ed. Charlotte, N.C.: MorningStar Publications, 1997.

_____. *The Watchmen: Being Prepared and Preparing the Way for Messiah.* Washington, D.C.: Progressive Vision International, 1998.

Hocken, Peter. *The Glory and the Shame: Reflections on the 20th Century Outpouring of the Holy Spirit.* Guildford, England: Eagle, 1994.

Intrater, Asher. *What Does the Bible Really Say about the Land?* Grand Prairie, Tex.: Maoz Israel Publishing, 2006.

_____. *Who Ate Lunch with Abraham?* Frederick, Md.: Review Israel Media, 2011.

Juster, Dan. *The Irrevocable Calling: Israel's Role As a Light to the Nations.* Clarksville, Md.: Lederer Books, 2006.

_____. *Jewish Roots: Understanding Your Jewish Faith*. Shippensburg, Penn.: Destiny Image, 2013.

_____. *One People, Many Tribes: A Primer on Church History from a Messianic Jewish Perspective*. Clarence, N.Y.: Kairos, 1999.

_____. *Revelation: The Passover Key*. Shippensburg, Penn.: Destiny Image, 1991.

Juster, Dan and Keith Intrader. *Israel, the Church and the Last Days*. Shippensburg, Penn.: Destiny Image, 2003.

Kjaer-Hansen, Kai. *Joseph Rabinowitz and the Messianic Movement: The Herzl of Jewish Christianity*. Grand Rapids, Mich.: Wm. B. Eerdmans, 1995.

Kjaer-Hansen, Kai, and Bodil F. Skjott. *Facts and Myths About the Messianic Congregations in Israel*. Jerusalem: United Christian Council in Israel in cooperation with the Caspari Center for Biblical and Jewish Studies, 1999.

Lightle, Steve. *Exodus II: Let My People Go*. Kingwood, Tex.: Hunter Books, 1983.

Murray, Iain H. *The Puritan Hope: Revival and the Interpretation of Prophecy*. Carlisle, Penn.: The Banner of Truth Trust, 1998.

Otis, George Jr. *The Last of the Giants*. Tarrytown, N.Y.: Chosen Books, Fleming H. Revell, 1991.

Pritz, Ray A. *Nazarene Jewish Christianity: From the End of the New Testament Period until Its Disappearance in the Fourth Century*. 1988. Reprint. Jerusalem: The Magnus Press, Hebrew University, 1992.

Richardson, Joel. *When a Jew Rules the World: What the Bible Really Says about Israel in the Plan of God*. Washington, D.C.: WND Books, 2015.

Rosen, Ruth. *Jewish Doctors Meet the Great Physician*. San Francisco, Calif.: Purple Pomegranate Productions, 1998.

_____. *Testimonies of Jews Who Believe in Jesus*. San Francisco, Calif.: Purple Pomegranate Productions, 1992.

Roth, Sid. *There Must Be Something More: The Spiritual Rebirth of a Jew*. Brunswick, Ga.: MV Press, 1994.

_____. *They Thought for Themselves*. Brunswick, Ga.: MV Press, 1996.

Scheller, Gustav. *Operation Exodus: Prophecy Being Fulfilled*. Kent, England: Sovereign World Limited, 1998.

Shishkoff, Eitan. *What About Us? The End-Time Calling of Gentiles in Israel's Revival*. Bedford, Tex.: Burkhart Books, 2013.

Stern, David H. *Complete Jewish Bible: An English Version of the Tanakh (Old Testament) and B'rit Hadashah (New Testament)*. Clarksville, Md.: Jewish New Testament Publications, 1998.

_____. *Messianic Jewish Manifesto*. Clarksville, Md.: Jewish New Testament Publications, 1988.

_____. *Restoring the Jewishness of the Gospel*. Jerusalem: Jewish New Testament Publications, 1988.

Telchin, Stan. *Betrayed!* Grand Rapids, Mich.: Chosen Books, 2007.

Teplinsky, Sandra. *Out of the Darkness: The Untold Story of Jewish Revival in the Former Soviet Union*. Jacksonville Beach, Fla.: Hear O Israel Publishing, 1998.

_____ *Why Still Care about Israel? The Sanctity of Covenant, Moral Justice and Prophetic Blessing*. Minneapolis, Chosen Books, 2013.

Urbach, Eliezer. *Out of the Fury: The Incredible Odyssey of Eliezer Urbach*. Charlotte, N.C.: Chosen People Ministries, 1987.

Wolff, Robert F., editor. *Awakening the One New Man*. Shippensburg, Penn.: Destiny Image Publishers, 2011.

Appendix C

Statement of Repentance
to the Jewish People
in America and
the Nations of the World[1]

Dear Respected Friends in the Jewish Community who share in our common faith in the G-d of Abraham, Isaac, and Jacob,

Something is happening in our generation that we deem to be motivated by the Almighty. People of different ethnic backgrounds and national origins are acknowledging the sins of past generations against each other in a desire for reconciliation and peace. The sons and daughters of former slave traders are taking upon themselves the sins of their forebears and confessing these sins to the sons and daughters of former slaves. You may be aware that a "Reconciliation Walk" was taken some years ago between Europe and Jerusalem by a group of Christians who were confessing the sins and devastation of the Crusaders.

We know that the Jewish people throughout the centuries have borne the greatest discrimination, the worst persecution, and the most barbaric atrocities of all. We, too, have read the histories. We are aware that much of this has been done by Christians or by those who called themselves Christians, sometimes while calling upon the name of Christ. This is a grotesque misrepresentation of the One who is called the Prince of Peace and who called us to love and worship our Heavenly Father, and to love our neighbor as ourselves. Though the Scriptures we call the New Testament have exhorted us to love, respect and exercise mercy towards you, the ancient people of G-d, and G-d's chosen people to this day, we and our forefathers in the Christian faith have rebelled against that command and have acted out of fear, prejudice, hatred, and jealousy. Those who have not so acted have acquiesced by their silence during the times of crusades, pogroms, and finally in the terrifying holocaust.

Nor are we Christian believers in the United States without our own share in this guilt. Not only are many of us descended from the perpetrators of these crimes, but our forefathers stood by without registering complaint when, in the years of the reign of horror in Europe, Jewish refugees were turned away from our shores. Our forefathers turned their eyes away from the death plight of the European Jewish community. Even in recent years, some in the Christian community have often stood in apathy as synagogues have been torched, cemeteries desecrated, and Jewish homes and businesses vandalized.

We grieve over these crimes against you, our Jewish brothers and sisters, and in the spirit of Daniel, who confessed the sins of former generations, we confess these horrors as sins and renounce them. We understand from our reading of the Prophet Zechariah that a time will yet come when the whole world turns against Israel. Should such a thing come to pass, many of us want to be numbered with those few Gentile Christians through the centuries who have risked their lives to protect you. We commit ourselves to standing with you in the strength of G-d, whatever the cost.

Notes

Introduction

1. The word *Christian* appears only three times in the apostolic writings (Acts 11:26, 26:28, and 1 Peter 4:16), each time used by others, not by the believers themselves.

Chapter 1: The Beginning of the End

1. A revolt against the Romans took place in AD 132, after the Roman Emperor Hadrian established a new city in Jerusalem and built in it a temple to Jupiter. The Bar Kokhba revolt is named after Simeon bar Koseva, later called Kokhba and thought by some to be the Messiah, who drove out the Romans. The designation *Kokhba* is thought to have been an allusion to the Numbers 24:17 reference to the "star" coming out of Judah, a Messianic reference. The revolt was short-lived, ending in a Roman victory in AD 134. ("Bar Kokhba" and "The Bar Kokhba Revolt," *Encyclopaedia Judaica* [Jerusalem: Judaica Multimedia, 1997], CDROM.)

2. If the vote were taken today, it would be hard to find a single nation that would approve Israel's statehood. Even the United States is pressuring her to make concessions for peace with nations who have vowed to drive her into the sea.

3. There was one brief interval in 164 BC when Judas Maccabaeus and his forces controlled Jerusalem, but it was only a matter of time before the Romans returned.

Chapter 2: The "Greater Riches" World Revival

1. This and all other statistics quoted in this chapter are taken from articles on world evangelism in the January 1993, January 1996 and January 1999 issues

211

of *Charisma*; from Bill and Amy Stearns, *Catch the Vision 2000* (Minneapolis, Minn.: Bethany House Publishers, 1991); and from a teaching tape by Loren Cunningham (founder and for many years director of Youth With A Mission), speaking at MorningStar Conference, Charlotte, North Carolina, and released as MorningStar's tape of the month in June 1998. Loren Cunningham often cites the Lausanne Task Force statistics.

2. Floyd McClung, ed., *Light the Window: Praying Through the Nations of the 10/40 Window* (Seattle: YWAM Publishing, 1999), 98.

3. Joel Rosenberg in the Foreword to Tass Saada, *Once an Arafat Man* (Carol Stream, Ill.: Tyndale House, 2008).

4. Iain H. Murray, *The Puritan Hope: A Study in Revival and the Interpretation of Prophecy* (1971; reprint, Carlisle, Penn.: Banner of Truth, 1998), 75.

5. Ibid., 72.

6. Ibid., 100.

7. Ibid., 155.

8. Handley C. G. Moule, ed., "The Epistle of St. Paul to the Romans," *Expositor's Bible, A Complete Exposition of the Bible in Six Volumes with Index*, vol. 5 (Grand Rapids, Mich.: Wm. B. Eerdmans Publishing Co., 1956), 590.

9. Andrew Bonar, *Memoir and Remains of Robert Murray M'Cheyne* (1844; reprint, Carlisle, Penn.: The Banner of Truth Trust, 1995), 192.

10. John R. Weinlick, *Count Zinzendorf: The Story of His Life and Leadership in the Renewed Moravian Church* (Nashville: Abingdon Press, 1956; Bethlehem, Penn.: The Moravian Church in America, 1984), 100.

11. C. H. Spurgeon, quoted in Murray, *The Puritan Hope*, 256.

12. Author Unknown, "The New Rebel Cry: Jesus Is Coming!" *Time*, June 21, 1971, 59.

13. Bill Bright, *The Coming Revival: America's Call to Fast, Pray, and Seek God's Face* (Orlando, Fla.: Newlife Publications, 1995), n.p.

14. Howard Folz, "The Unfinished Task of World Evangelism," *Charisma*, January 1999, 50.

15. John Lindner, "India: Reaching Hidden People," *Charisma*, January 2000, 66.

16. George Otis Jr., *The Last of the Giants* (Tarrytown, N.Y.: Fleming H. Revell, 1991), 157, 158.

17. Folz, "The Unfinished Task," 47.

18. Samaa Habib and Bodie Thoene, *Face to Face with Jesus, A Former Muslim's Extraordinary Journey to Heaven and Encounter with the God of Love* (Grand Rapids, Mich.: Chosen Books, 2014).

Chapter 3: Israel—A Nation of Priests

1. S. I. McMillen, *None of These Diseases* (1963; reprint, Old Tappan, N.J.: Fleming H. Revell, 1979), 12–16.

2. Ibid., 17, 18.

3. Ibid., 20.

4. A careful reading of Scripture seems to indicate that Jesus was born, not at Christmas, but during the Feast of Tabernacles. John the Baptist's father,

Zechariah, was a priest in the division of Abijah (see Luke 1:5). Abijah's division was the eighth out of 24, thus the latter part of the fourth biblical month that begins on the first day of Nisan, fourteen days before Passover (see Exodus 12:1). Thus, the announcement to Zechariah that his wife, Elizabeth, would become pregnant would have come during that last half of the fourth month. In the sixth month of Elizabeth's pregnancy—the latter part of the tenth biblical month—Gabriel appeared to Miriam (Mary) announcing that she would bear the Messiah (see Luke 1:35). If Jesus was born nine months following Gabriel's visit, then Jesus would be born nineteen months after the announcement to Zechariah, thus in the latter part of the seventh following year. The Feast of Tabernacles begins on the fifteenth day of the seventh month and lasts for seven days (see Leviticus 23:34).

5. Leslie B. Flynn, *What the Church Owes the Jew* (Carlsbad, Calif.: Magnus Press, 1998), 1.

6. Ibid., 2.

7. Rabbi Joseph Telushkin, *Jewish Wisdom* (New York: William Morrow & Company, 1994), 498.

Chapter 4: The Targeted Annihilation

1. Marty Waldman is one of the leaders of today's Messianic Jewish community. He has served as president of the Union of Messianic Jewish Synagogues in the United States and is the spiritual leader of the Baruch HaShem congregation of believers in Dallas, Texas.

2. Eitan Shishkoff presently serves as the spiritual leader of the *Ohalei Rachamim* (Tents of Mercy) synagogue in the Kryot, north of Haifa in Israel.

3. Judas Maccabaeus, whose name is immortalized in the intertestamental *Books of the Maccabees,* assumed the leadership of the great Jewish revolt against the Syrian leader, Antiochus Epiphanes. In 164 BC, Judas took the city of Jerusalem, purified the defiled Temple and instituted a festival of eight days, which became the permanent festival of *Hanukkah.* For one brief interlude, Israel had overthrown the Syrian forces.

4. Michael Brown, *Our Hands Are Stained with Blood* (Shippensburg, Penn.: Destiny Image, 1992), 11, quoted from Malcolm Hay, *The Roots of Christian Anti-Semitism* (New York: Liberty Press, 1981), 27.

5. Ibid., 14, 15, quoted from Frank Ephraim Talmage, ed., *Disputation and Dialogue: Readings in the Jewish-Christian Encounter* (New York: Ktav/Anti-Defamation League of B'nai B'rit, 1975), 34–36.

6. Ibid., 15.

Chapter 5: The Early Jewish "Church"

1. David H. Stern, *The Complete Jewish Bible: An English Version of the Tanakh (Old Testament) and B'rit Hadashah (New Testament)* (Clarksville, Md.: Jewish New Testament Publications, 1998).

2. Russell L. Resnik, *The Root and the Branches: Jewish Identity in Messiah* (Albuquerque, N.Mex.: Adat Yeshua, 1997), 72–73.

3. Ibid., 80.

4. David H. Stern was born in Los Angeles in 1935, the great-grandson of two of the city's first twenty Jews. He earned a Ph.D. in economics at Princeton University and was a professor at UCLA. In 1972 he came to faith in Yeshua; he received a master of divinity degree from Fuller Theological Seminary and did graduate work at the University of Judaism. Dr. Stern taught Fuller Seminary's first course in Judaism and Christianity, organized Messianic Jewish conferences and leaders' meetings and served as an officer of the Messianic Jewish Alliance of America. In 1979, the Stern family—his wife, Martha Frankel, and their two children—made *aliyah* (immigrated to Israel) and now reside in Jerusalem. Dr. Stern is the author of several books and the translator of *The Complete Jewish Bible,* as described above.

5. Ray A. Pritz, *Nazarene Jewish Christianity: From the End of the New Testament Period Until Its Disappearance in the Fourth Century* (1988; reprint, Jerusalem: Magnus Press, The Hebrew University, 1992) gives a well-documented history of these early centuries.

Chapter 6: The "Gentilizing" of the Church

1. Origen, *Against Celsus*, quoted in Ray A. Pritz, *Nazarene Jewish Christianity: From the End of the New Testament Period Until Its Disappearance in the Fourth Century* (1988; reprint, Jerusalem: Magnus Press, The Hebrew University, 1992), 21.

2. Constantine, quoted in Dan Gruber, *The Church and the Jews* (Hanover, N.H.: Elijah Publishing, 1997), 35.

3. Ibid.

4. John Chrysostom, *Homilies on the Acts of the Apostles and the Epistle to the Romans,* from *A Select Library of the Nicene and Post-Nicene Fathers of the Christian Church,* vol. 11, ed. Philip Schaff (New York: The Christian Literature Company, 1889), 491.

5. Replacement Theology is the belief that God is finished with Israel and that the Gentile Church has now replaced her, that there is no future role for Israel and the Jewish people.

6. Canon VIII from the Second Nicene Council.

7. Martin Luther, *Commentary on the Epistle to the Romans,* trans. J. Theodore Mueller (Grand Rapids, Mich.: Zondervan Publishing House, 1954), n.p.

8. *Harper's Bible Dictionary,* 1985, s.v. "Israel."

9. *Thompson Chain Reference Bible,* 4th improved ed. (Indianapolis: B. B. Kirkbride Company, 1964).

10. David Chilton, *The Days of Vengeance: An Exposition of the Book of Revelation* (Fort Worth, Tex.: Dominion Press, 1984), 117.

11. One of the passages of Scripture occasionally mentioned in support of "Replacement Theology"—the belief that the Church has now replaced Israel—is in the conclusion of Paul's letter to the Galatians (6:16). In Paul's benediction, he says, "Peace and mercy to all who follow this rule, even to the Israel of God." The argument is that Paul is here referring to the Church as the "Israel of God." As a replacement for Israel? Who says? How does the "Israel

of God" suddenly mean the Church when it has meant the "Israel of God" since the days of Abraham, Isaac and Jacob!

At the very most, Paul may be including believing Gentiles, since he has assured the Roman believers that Gentiles are grafted into the Jewish olive root (see Romans 11:17–18). In his letter to the Romans, he is adamant that they have not replaced but share in the Jewish root (see 11:11–24). Now in this Galatian letter, Paul is continually emphasizing that law never has and never will save, that salvation and sanctification come through the finished work of the Messiah through the Holy Spirit, and that the Gentiles have never been placed under the same Mosaic requirements as Israel. But never does he suggest that God is finished with Israel.

After writing an entire letter warning against those who would require Gentiles to be Torah-observant (see Galatians 2:13–14) or even make Torah-observance a saving factor for Jews (see verses 15–16), he concludes by saying neither circumcision nor uncircumcision means anything; what counts is a new creation (see. 6:15). In other words, it's not Jewishness or Gentileness that save; it is the blood of Messiah.

Listen carefully to his benediction once again: "Peace and mercy to all who follow this rule" (6:16). Who are those who follow this rule? They are both the Gentile believers and Jewish believers—all who have come to faith through Messiah's finished work at the cross. But Paul's prayer for peace and mercy goes beyond only those who are already following this rule.

In true Jewish poetic style, he expands on his initial remarks. He is thinking of those who have yet to acknowledge their Messiah. He may be remembering the psalmist's admonition to "pray for the peace of Jerusalem" (Psalm 122:6) as he ponders the fate of his own countrymen. Isaiah's words—reminding all who call on the Lord to give themselves no rest and to give the Lord no rest until Jerusalem is established and made the praise of the earth—may be pulsating through his heart as he adds that final phrase, "even to the Israel of God." As a called apostle to the Gentiles, he may also be thinking of the countless Gentiles who will be grafted into the family by faith, sharing in the promises of Abraham through Israel's Promised Redeemer.

But in no way does Paul intimate that God is through with Israel and that the Church has taken her place. Nothing in Galatians or Romans or any of Paul's letters—or the letters of the other apostles, for that matter—can be so construed unless we have been culturally trained to think this way. May the Word speak for itself.

Chapter 7: Division—The DNA of the Gentile Church

1. *The World Book Encyclopedia,* 1962, s.v. "mutations."

2. Martin J. Waldman, "Reconciliation: A Jewish-Gentile Issue Facing the Church Today" (paper presented to the Network of Christian Ministries, December 1998), 9.

3. From the "Statement of Purpose, Toward Jerusalem Council II, 1997." Toward Jerusalem Council II is a steering committee of Jewish and Gentile believers who are targeting the time when the entire Gentile Church calls a second

council not unlike the council called in Acts 15. This time, however, it would be called to confess the sins of the Gentiles against the Jews and to welcome Jewish believers back into the family of their own Messiah. See Appendix C for a statement of repentance.

Chapter 8: Return to the Land

1. Israel was granted a certain land allotment for the State in the United Nations resolution of November 1947. The surrounding Arab nations did not honor that resolution, however, and went to war immediately upon the declaration of the State of Israel in May 1948. A few days later those same Arab nations were calling for a ceasefire, with Israel gaining additional land in this war they had neither initiated nor desired. A similar thing happened in the Six-Day War of June 1967. Shortly after war was declared, Syria, one of the chief aggressors, seeing that Israel was within firing range of her capital city of Damascus, sued for quick resolution. Egypt, in the same war, basically lost her complete air force in the early days of fighting. At the end of the war, Israel's landmass was several times larger than at the outset of the war. The Yom Kippur War of 1973 was no different, though Israel was less prepared for battle. Nevertheless, in every war with her neighbors, Israel's boundaries have increased. If she had not given back land for peace, she would today be many times larger than required by the original UN resolution.

2. For a complete account of Eliezer Urbach's story, see his book *Out of the Fury: The Incredible Odyssey of Eliezer Urbach* (Charlotte, N.C.: Chosen People Ministries, 1987).

3. The Hebrew Immigrant Aid Society is affiliated with Jewish committees in the United States.

4. Larry Collins and Dominique Lapierre, *O Jerusalem! Day by Day and Minute by Minute: The Historic Struggle for Jerusalem and the Birth of Israel* (New York: Simon and Schuster, 1972). The story of Dreyfus, Herzl and the Jewish nation is well told in this volume.

5. Ramon Bennett, *When Day and Night Cease* (Jerusalem: Arm of Salvation Press, 1992), 92.

6. Tom Hess, *Let My People Go! The Struggle of the Jewish People to Return to Israel*, 5th ed. (Charlotte, N.C.: MorningStar Publications, 1997), 174.

7. Bennett, *When Day and Night Cease*, 92.

8. Collins and Lapierre, *O Jerusalem!*, 187–190.

9. Bennett, *When Day and Night Cease*, 164.

10. Ibid., 165.

11. These statistics, reported by the Central Bureau of Statistics, are contained in a *Jerusalem Post* article (jpost.com) of December 30, 2014, entitled, "On the eve of 2015, Israel's population hits 8.3 million."

Chapter 9: The Awakening

1. In a subsequent visit only six months later, there were two hundred believers in this Jewish congregation!

2. Reuven Doron, *One New Man* (Cedar Rapids, Iowa: Embrace Israel, 1996), 47.

3. Julian Wagner, "The New Rebel Cry: Jesus Is Coming!" *Time* (June 21, 1971), 59.

4. "The Theology of Israel's Fiftieth Birthday," *Teaching from Zion* (Jerusalem: Netivyah Bible Instruction Ministry, 1998), 2.

5. Alan Cooperman, ed., "A Portrait of Jewish Americans," Pew Research, October 1, 2013, www.pewresearch.org.

6. Read the complete story in Gari Goldberg-Distefano, *An Unexpected Miracle* (Mustang, Okla.: Tate Publishing, 2014).

7. Read Stan and Ethel's complete story in his book *Betrayed* (Old Tappan, N.J.: Chosen Books, Fleming H. Revell, 1981).

8. Dr. Stracher's story is told in the book *Jewish Doctors Meet the Great Physician*, Ruth Rose, ed. (San Francisco, Calif.: Purple Pomegranate Productions, 1998), 55–68.

9. Ibid., 107–122.

Chapter 10: The Resurrected "Nazarenes"

1. Kai Kjaer-Hansen, *Joseph Rabinowitz and the Messianic Movement: The Herzl of Jewish Christianity* (Grand Rapids, Mich.: Wm. B. Eerdmans, 1995), 19.

2. Ibid., 74.

3. Ibid., 70.

4. Ibid., 104.

5. Ibid., 151–152.

6. Ibid., 5.

7. Peter Hocken, *The Glory and the Shame: Reflections on the 20th Century Outpouring of the Holy Spirit* (Guildford, England: Eagle, 1994), 160.

8. Kjaer-Hansen, *Joseph Rabinowitz and the Messianic Movement*, 233.

9. The founding of the Hebrew Christian Alliance in 1915 is mentioned in Michael Schiffman, *Return of the Remnant—The Rebirth of Messianic Judaism* (Baltimore, Md.: Lederer Messianic Publishers, 1992), 27.

10. For the complete story of the Chernoffs, see Yohanna Chernoff, *Born a Jew . . . Die a Jew: The Story of Martin Chernoff, a Pioneer in Messianic Judaism* (Hagerstown, Md.: EBED Publications, 1996).

11. David Rausch, quoted in Chernoff, *Born a Jew . . . Die a Jew*, 178.

12. Martin J. Waldman, "Reconciliation: A Jewish-Gentile Issue Facing the Church Today" (unpublished), 2.

13. Jonathan Bernis, "Have You Hugged a (Messianic) Jew Lately?" *Charisma*, April 1997, 68.

14. Kai Kjaer-Hansen and Bodil F. Skjott, *Facts and Myths About the Messianic Congregations in Israel* (Jerusalem: United Christian Council in Israel in cooperation with the Caspari Center for Biblical and Jewish Studies, 1999), 16.

15. This is an estimate given in the October 29, 2013, edition of *Charisma* magazine.

16. Gary Thomas, "The Return of the Jewish Church," *Christianity Today*, September 1998, 63.

17. Gary Thomas, "The Lord Is Gathering His People," *Charisma*, April 1997, 54.

18. For more information on our own ministry, go to calebcompany.org, don finto.org and calebpublications.org.

19. Chernoff, *Born a Jew . . . Die a Jew,* 183–197.

20. Dan Juster, introduction to *Jewish Roots: A Foundation of Biblical Theology* (Shippensburg, Penn.: Destiny Image Publishers, 1995).

21. For more information, go to firm.org.il.

22. Rick Joyner, "The Messianic Movement," *Morning Star Journal,* vol. 10 (Charlotte, N.C.: MorningStar Publications, 1999), 42.

23. Eitan Shishkoff, "I Love Jesus, but Don't Call Me Christian!" *Charisma,* January 25, 2013, http://www.charismamag.com/spirit/world-religions/11939-terms-of-offense.

Chapter 11: Jew and Gentile—"One New Man"

1. Joel Richardson, *When a Jew Rules the World: What the Bible Really Says about Israel in the Plan of God* (Washington, D.C.: WND Books, 2015).

2. John Mason Neal, *"Psalteriolum Cantionum Catholicarum."* The words of this Latin hymn, composed in 1710, were written in 1851.

Chapter 13: The Final Exodus

1. This account was taken from the personal testimony of Sudanese people now living in our city.

2. I have traveled to Uganda, held seminars for young preachers who have spoken of these atrocities and have lived in communities with people who were acquainted with these happenings in Uganda during the Idi Amin reign.

3. These incidents are recorded by a Chinese brother who bicycled for six months through China to collect the stories of the Chinese revival (Danyon, *Lilies Among Thorns* [Kent, England: Sovereign World, Ltd.; distributed in the U.S. by Gospel Light, 1991]).

4. Tadesa (an Ethiopian brother), interview by author (April 1999).

Chapter 14: Blessed to Be a Blessing

1. A Channel 1 interview broadcast in Hebrew on December 25, 1999, on the program *Popolitika,* in which three Israelis spoke of their impressions of Yeshua. In addition to Professor Ravitsky, a leader in Israeli television stated that he hated Jesus and blamed Him for the murder of his parents—until he had a chance to read the New Testament. It was then he realized that he had to separate the history between Judaism and Christianity from the person of Yeshua. He encouraged all Israelis to read the New Testament. The head of all Israeli security forces suggested that the teachings of Yeshua are more appropriate for Israelis today than the teachings of the rabbis.

2. For many stories of preparation for the coming exodus, see Steve Lightle, *Exodus II: Let My People Go, Section II* (Kingwood, Tex.: Hunter Books, 1983).

3. Tom Hess, *Let My People Go: The Struggle of the Jewish People to Return to Israel,* 5th ed. (Charlotte, N.C.: MorningStar Publications, 1997), n.p.

4. Ibid., 30.

5. Ibid., 70, 75.

6. Ibid., 109.

7. Gustav Scheller, *Operation Exodus: Prophecy Being Fulfilled* (Kent, England: Sovereign World, 1998).

8. Larry Collins and Dominique Lapierre, *O Jerusalem! Day by Day and Minute by Minute: The Historic Struggle for Jerusalem and the Birth of Israel* (New York: Simon and Schuster, 1972), 162–166.

Appendix C: Statement of Repentance to the Jewish People in America and the Nations of the World

1. Used by permission of Generals of Intercession, P.O. Box 49788, Colorado Springs, CO 80949; fax: 719-535-0884; website: www.generals.org.

Don Finto served as pastor of Belmont Church in Nashville for more than 25 years. He continues to serve as a pastor to pastors, and he has become actively involved with the resurrected community of Jewish believers in Jesus, both in the United States and Israel. He started the Caleb Company ministry in 1996 in order to "equip God's people with His heart and purpose for Israel and the nations." He and his wife, Martha Ann, have three children, seven grandchildren and five great-grandchildren.

If you would like to know more about the Caleb Company ministry, training schools, speaking engagements and trips to Israel, or Jewish-related ministries, contact us at www.calebcompany.org.

For other resources, go to www.calebpublications.org.

If you would like to connect with Don Finto personally, go to www.donfinto.org or contact Don in care of The Caleb Company, P.O. Box 493, Thompsons Station, TN 37179.